The South and the Transformation of U.S. Politics

The South and the Transformation of U.S. Politics

CHARLES S. BULLOCK III
SUSAN A. MACMANUS
JEREMY D. MAYER
MARK J. ROZELL

OXFORD
UNIVERSITY PRESS

OXFORD
UNIVERSITY PRESS

Oxford University Press is a department of the University of Oxford. It furthers
the University's objective of excellence in research, scholarship, and education
by publishing worldwide. Oxford is a registered trade mark of Oxford University
Press in the UK and certain other countries.

Published in the United States of America by Oxford University Press
198 Madison Avenue, New York, NY 10016, United States of America.

© Oxford University Press 2019

CIP data is on file at the Library of Congress
ISBN 978-0-19-006592-8 (pbk.)
ISBN 978-0-19-006591-1 (hbk.)

Contents

Preface

This book is a collaboration that began with the four of us presenting our research at an academic conference of the British Association of American Studies in London on the fiftieth anniversary of the profoundly important events of 1968. We offered a panel on how the South had changed and transformed U.S. politics from 1968 to 2018. The common themes and compatibility of our findings encouraged us to expand on our original presentations to write more fully developed analyses for this volume. MacManus wrote on demographics, Bullock on partisanship, Rozell on the religious right, and Mayer on President Donald J. Trump's southern electoral appeal. Although race underlies all of the above, we determined that the volume must have a chapter separately devoted to that topic (Bullock and Rozell). Each of us took the lead on our individual chapters and we then collaborated and agreed on all of the content in the volume. An introduction to the politics of the South and its transformations (Bullock) and a conclusion summarizing major findings (Rozell) complete the volume.

Analyzing and explaining the transformation of U.S. politics since the explosive events of 1968 require particular attention to the South—the states of the former Confederacy. Indeed, a strong case can be made that the South has had the greatest impact on the transformation of U.S. politics and government. Since 1968 we have seen the demise of the "sold (Democratic) South" and the rise of the Republican-dominated South, the rise of the largely southern white evangelical religious right movement, and vast demographic changes that have vastly altered the political landscape of the region and national politics. And overriding all of these changes is the major constant of southern politics—race.

The strong support shown for Donald J. Trump in the primaries and general election of 2016 demonstrates the ongoing centrality of race in Southern politics. What would have been disqualifying for other candidates was accepted in the case of Trump in part because no presidential candidate since George Wallace has so deftly captured white rage against black progress. The Bible Belt white South put its nearly unified support behind a man who had been pro-choice and pro-gun control, owned strip clubs, appeared in softcore porn movies, and was publicly unfaithful to at least two of his three wives. Moreover, he displayed an extraordinary level of ignorance of basic shibboleths and norms of the Christian faith, belonged to no church, and had no born-again faith, factors that had once been important to white Southern voters.

Nonetheless, demographic trends portend another major shift in the politics of the South that will have profound impacts on U.S. government and politics. Just as the South shifted from solid Democratic to Republican dominated, it now appears that the trends will shift some of the region back to the Democratic Party. That is already happening in Rim South states such as Virginia and North Carolina, and somewhat in certain deep South states such as Georgia and eventually Texas.

The chapters in this book explain how the South has fundamentally changed in the past half-century and how that has dramatically altered U.S. national politics. The first chapter sets the framework for the book. The second presents an overview of the demographic changes in the South, the third is on the partisan changes in the South, the fourth covers the changing politics of race in the region; the fifth describes the rise of the evangelical right in the region, and the sixth presents the election and early presidential term of Donald J. Trump as the culmination of the trends examined in the earlier chapters. A brief conclusion summarizes key findings and speculates about the future of the South's influence on the national political landscape.

1

How the South Has Changed and Its Impact on National Politics

When Martin Luther King was assassinated in Memphis in 1968, in many ways the South that he was in the process of transforming remained more like that of his father's or grandfather's generation than the South today. Congress had yet to pass an open housing act. A number of Southern legislative chambers and many local governments, even in communities with substantial African American populations, had no black elected officials. The higher positions in the labor force, both private and public, were almost exclusively white. To the extent that minorities had been hired, they tended to be as maids or janitors.

The South of half a century ago was also, as it had always been, almost exclusively a black and white region with few if any other ethnic groups present, except in south Texas and Miami. Although *Brown v. Board of Education* (1954) had ruled that racially segregated schools were unconstitutional and must be eliminated, very few African American children attended schools having any white students. Most Southern communities had schools as segregated in 1968 as they had been in 1948 or 1908. Born-again Christians were far and away dominant in terms of religion but these denominations were largely apolitical.

In 1968 Alabama's George Wallace and other politicians who used the Alabama governor as their model won office by promising not simply to hold the line against increasing federal pressures for equality but vowed that they would return the South to an earlier time. Rare indeed was the Southern public official who would publicly support the Civil Rights Act of 1964 or the Voting Rights Act passed the next year. Without providing extensive detail, the segregationists vowed that they could block federal demands that minorities be treated equally. The rallying cry of "segregation now, segregation tomorrow, segregation forever" sufficed to win Wallace five states' Electoral College votes in 1968.[1]

A half century ago, almost all of the politics in the region continued to be fought out within the Democratic Party, much as it had been for the previous century. Only in presidential elections had Republicans enjoyed much success. In 1968 Republican governors and senators were rare. Republican caucuses in state legislatures were tiny and ineffectual. The Democratic primary or runoff usually determined who held office, especially at the local level. Ideologically the Democratic Party was a huge tent whose members ranged from arch conservatives to progressives. The region's members of Congress were often out of step with their Northern co-partisans, and frequently most Southern Democrats voted with Republicans against reformist initiatives. With huge majorities gained in the 1964 election, Lyndon B. Johnson (LBJ) succeeded in pushing a range of progressive ideas into law including the Voting Rights Act, Medicare, and Medicaid, but this was the exception as the Conservative Coalition of Southern Democrats and Republicans enjoyed great success in most congresses (Brady and Bullock 1980; Shelley 1983).

Fifty Years Later

Today much that King knew has changed although there remain some features he would recognize. The South that for a century was the foundation upon which the Democratic presidential candidacies and congressional control rested has shifted 180 degrees and become the most loyal component of the Republican Party. The region's Republicans have played an oversized role in the success their party has had in controlling Congress for most of the last quarter century. As of 2018, every Southern legislative chamber had a Republican majority and eight state houses had Republican governors.

The much-reduced Democratic Party is now largely a home for minorities, whose ancestors often could not vote and held no offices fifty years ago. In 2018 two-thirds of the South's Democratic delegation to

Congress consists of minority members and while that year's elections sent new three white Democrats to Congress from Virginia and one each from Florida, Texas, and South Carolina, Georgia and Texas added an African American to their delegations. Two Latinas replaced Republicans in Florida, and in Texas two Latinas succeeded Anglo Democrats. Every Southern state except for Arkansas and Tennessee has at least one African American representing it in Congress led by Texas with six and Georgia with five black representatives.[2] Across the Deep South, Democratic ranks in the state legislature are over-whelmingly black.[3] In some state legislative chambers blacks' share of the seats approximates the black share of the adult population. Trial courts in the urban South have African American judges. Virtually every city, county, and school district with a substantial minority population now has black representation on its governing body. Growing numbers of Hispanics and some Asians are winning offices, with the former group especially prevalent in Texas where they hold seven congressional seats, and Florida.

The region, which for decades experienced outmigration, now boasts some of the nation's most explosive growth. Texas, which a century ago had a population equal to that of Missouri, is now the second-most populous state in the union. Florida, which in 1940 was the least populous state in the South, has overtaken New York to become number three in population. Georgia, which a half century ago had a population similar in size to Wisconsin, has passed Michigan to be the eighth most populous with North Carolina number nine. The region accounts for the largest component of the Electoral College.

Within this growing population comes greater diversity. Hispanics outnumber African Americans in Texas and Florida, and by a substantial margin in the Lone Star State. Georgia, which had no Hispanic population a half century ago, is now approximately 10 percent Hispanic. The region is also attracting Asians, and Georgia now has an Asian on its Court of Appeals as well as in its General Assembly.

The region, often referred to as the Bible Belt, like the rest of the nation, is seeing declining church attendance, particularly in urban areas and among millennials. But even as church attendance becomes less universal, Evangelicals gain political influence as the most loyal component of the GOP. The social conservativism that frequently accompanied the religious fundamentalism that dominated the region is also beginning to change. Southern cities increasingly allow alcohol consumption on Sunday and the region, which eagerly embraced constitutional amendments banning same-sex marriage in the mid-2000s, now sees the LGBT (lesbian, gay, bisexual, transgender) community represented in the ranks of its elected officials. In 2017, a transgendered Virginian made national news when she defeated one of the most socially conservative and long-serving Republicans in the House of Delegates.

Growth in the South has been uneven with Southern cities' magnetism attracting people from the region's hinterland and also from across the country and abroad. Atlanta is a mecca for black professionals whose mansions cover the city's west side with subdivisions spreading further out in all directions. Austin, Atlanta, Charlotte, and Nashville are among the destinations most favored by millennials. The availability of good-paying jobs and a dynamic social scene add to the allure of a climate that allows yearlong golf, tennis, and hiking.

A New Dichotomy among Southern States

V.O. Key (1949) saw race as the defining issue for the South. His sage assessment is often quoted:

> In its grand outline the politics of the South revolves around the position of the Negro. It is at times interpreted as a politics of cotton, as a politics of free trade, as a politics of agrarian poverty, or as a politics of planter and plutocrat. Although such interpretations have a superficial validity, in the last analysis the major peculiarities of southern politics go back to the Negro. Whatever phase of the southern political process one seeks to understand, sooner or later the trail of inquiry leads to the Negro. (p. 5)

The areas with the heaviest concentrations of black populations tended to set the tone in terms of policies of racial suppression, which constituted a major reason for the region's loyalty to the Democratic Party, which for decades turned a blind eye to the South's peculiar institutions.

The presence of African Americans had an influence throughout the region save for the mountains where few if any blacks lived. Nonetheless there was variation. The concentration of African Americans played a role in the division of the region into the Rim or Peripheral South and the Deep South. The Deep South states had the largest black populations, were more agrarian, and were the areas in which the Democratic Party was most dominant. When all the Rim States but Arkansas turned against the New York, Catholic, anti-prohibitionist Al Smith in 1928, the Deep South remained unmoved with South Carolina giving Smith 91 percent support and Louisiana and Mississippi each going for the Democrat by margins of more than three-to-one.

Some Rim South states, particularly Tennessee, North Carolina, and to an extent Virginia, had traces of a Republican Party even when V.O. Key published his groundbreaking *Southern Politics* in 1949. Rim South voters began to show an interest in the GOP a decade or so earlier than their Deep South cousins. Most Rim South states began voting Republican for president with Dwight D. Eisenhower and his coattails brought Republicans to Congress and state legislative chambers. The first victories in statewide offices for the GOP came in the Rim South. School desegregation also began earlier in Rim South cities than in the Deep South.

While race undeniably remains a major consideration in the region, as in much of the country, today a new element separates parts of the South. States that over the last half century have outpaced the national growth rate to the extent that they added congressional seats are becoming less like the states that have grown in step with the nation or have actually lost representation in Congress. The Growth States have stronger economies and higher family incomes, and seem poised for change in terms of partisanship but also policy. Growth in population and prosperity characterizes the Atlantic Seaboard. The people moving to these states along with Texas display a greater diversity than the black-white dichotomy that traditionally characterized the region. These new populations help make their neighborhoods more like growth areas elsewhere in the nation with mixtures of cultures from around the nation and the world. This variety undermines the parochialism that characterized much of the South for generations. It also results in a larger share of the population willing and sometimes even eager to accept change. The change incorporates a greater tolerance for ideas and practices and this has led to a rebound of the Democratic Party. Two states—Texas and Florida—have grown at warp speed to become the second and third largest states in the nation. Their growth continues unabated with the expectation that each will add at least two members of Congress following the 2020 census.

In addition to the relocation of Northern Democrats, often retirees, to the state's east coast, Florida has experienced an explosion in the Hispanic population not just in Miami but also in the Orlando area. The idea that most Hispanics in Florida had escaped from Castro's Cuba is passé. Many new residents have ties to Puerto Rico, with some coming directly from the island while others have relocated from the Northeast. Regardless of their last address, they can register and vote since they are American citizens. Even in Miami, the non-Cuban component outnumbers those of Cuban heritage and some younger Cuban Americans are joining other Hispanics in the Democratic column. In 2018 two Miami seats that Republicans had held with the exception of a single term since their creation elected Democrats. In the 27th District former University of Miami president Donna Shalala (D) replaced Ileana Ros-Lehtinen (R) who had been the first Cuban American to go to Congress.

While Texas and Florida have had phenomenal growth, Table 1.1 shows four other states have grown more rapidly than the nation as a whole over the latest half century. Included here are Georgia, North Carolina, South Carolina, and Virginia. Each of these states has gained at least one member of Congress since 1949–1950 and Georgia has added four beginning with the 1990 census. These four plus Florida and Texas will be referred to as the Growth States in this volume. Note that they include two Deep South states. The remaining states will be referred to as the Stagnant States. None of the Stagnant States has more representation in Congress today than in the middle of the twentieth century. Arkansas and Mississippi have lost three seats each while Alabama and Louisiana have declined by two each.

The Growth States have by definition succeeded in attracting new residents. The attraction has been so strong that most of those who live in Florida and Virginia are not native to the state. Each of the other

Table 1.1. Congressional representation

State	1949–1950	1959–1960	1969–1970	1979–1980	1989–1990	1999–2000	2009–2010	2018	Change
Alabama	9	9	8	7	7	7	7	7	-2
Arkansas	7	6	4	4	4	4	4	4	-3
Florida	6	8	12	15	19	23	25	27	21
Georgia	10	10	10	10	10	11	13	14	4
Louisiana	8	8	8	8	8	7	7	6	-2
Mississippi	7	6	5	5	5	5	4	4	-3
N. Carolina	12	12	11	11	11	12	13	13	1
S. Carolina	6	6	6	6	6	6	6	7	1
Tennessee	10	9	9	8	9	9	9	9	-1
Texas	21	22	23	24	27	30	32	36	15
Virginia	9	10	10	10	10	11	11	11	2

Source: Created by the author.

Growth States has a larger share of its residents not born in the state than any of the Stagnant States. At the other extreme, 78 percent of those who have remained in Louisiana despite a depressed economy and Hurricane Katrina were born in the state. In the Alabama and Mississippi populations more than 70 percent are natives.

Population growth is associated with various measures of economic success. Indeed a strong economy is essential to attracting new residents. The economies of the Growth States are surging. The 2015 median household income in each of the Growth States exceeds that for any of the other five states. The highest median income, $65,015, places Virginia eighth in the nation. At the other extreme, Arkansas and Mississippi place 49th and 50th, respectively as shown in Table 1.2. The Growth States also outpace each of the other states in terms of the share of their adult populations who have a baccalaureate degree while the other five states have populations with larger shares than the Growth States of adults with a high school diploma or less as reported in Table 1.3. The separation between the Growth and Stagnant states

Table 1.2. Median family incomes, 1970 and 2015

State	1970		2015	
	$ Amount	Rank	$ Amount	Rank
Alabama	7,263	48	43,623	47
Arkansas	6,271	49	41,371	49
Florida	8,261	35	47,507	38
Georgia	8,165	37	49,620	31
Louisiana	7,527	43	45,047	44
Mississippi	6,068	50	39,665	50
North Carolina	7,770	40	46,868	41
South Carolina	7,620	42	45,483	42
Tennessee	7,447	45	45,219	43
Texas	8,486	33	53,207	23
Virginia	9,045	25	65,015	8

Source: Created by the author.

Table 1.3. Education levels

	College Degree or More (%)	High School or Less (%)
Growth States		
Florida	27.3	42.6
Georgia	28.8	43.0
North Carolina	28.3	40.9
South Carolina	25.8	44.2
Texas	27.6	43.3
Virginia	36.4	36.5
Stagnant States		
Alabama	23.5	46.8
Arkansas	21.1	50.2
Louisiana	22.5	50.5
Mississippi	20.6	47.9
Tennessee	24.9	47.5

Source: Created by the author.

is greater on the education measures, especially in percent with high school or less, than on median income.

The Growth States, as a group, differ from the remainder of the South in terms of partisanship. Until recently the entire region was a scarlet swath in which the blue dots were too small to impact statewide contests. As recently as 2004, every state lined up behind the Republican presidential nominee. Population growth has been associated with partisan change with the most dramatic change coming in Virginia, which, at least in terms of statewide politics, has become a Democratic state. Elsewhere the Democratic Party, while still the minority, has made some headway although the extent to which it can successfully challenge the GOP varies among these six states.

If we look just at statewide contests, we see that the region's leader in income and education, Virginia, has voted for the Democrat in the last three presidential elections, the last two gubernatorial elections, and the last four senatorial elections. All three of its statewide constitutional officers are Democrats. Following a color coding, Florida and North Carolina are purple as their statewide contests are hotly contested, and over the last decade they voted Democratic at least once for president and senator. In the other three states Democrats have yet to score significant victories, but at least in Georgia, the GOP margins continue to shrink. In Georgia the margin by which top-of-the-ticket Republicans won has declined from half a million a decade ago to 200,000 in 2014 and 2016 to 55,000 in 2018.

Results from the 2016 presidential election clearly distinguished between the two sets of states. Table 1.4 arranges states by the share of the vote won by Donald J. Trump going from Virginia, which went for Hillary Clinton by 5.4 percentage points, to Alabama, which Trump carried by 28 points. Growth States tended to be competitive with the outcome in four decided by less than six points. Only in South Carolina did the margin in a Growth State exceed ten points. In contrast, Trump's advantage in the Stagnant States was at 20 percentage

Table 1.4. Partisan competitiveness in the 2016 presidential election

	Trump%	Clinton%	Margin
Growth States			
Virginia	44.8	50.2	5.4D
Florida	49.0	47.8	1.2R
North Carolina	50.5	46.8	3.7R
Georgia	51.0	45.9	5.1R
Texas	52.5	43.5	9.0R
South Carolina	54.9	40.7	14.2R
Stagnant States			
Mississippi	57.9	40.1	17.8R
Louisiana	58.1	38.4	19.7R
Arkansas	60.6	33.7	26.9R
Tennessee	61.1	34.9	26.2R
Alabama	62.7	34.7	28.0R

Source: Created by the author.

points or above except in Mississippi where the large black population held him to a 17.8 percentage points win.

Some high-profile elections in Growth States remained extremely competitive in 2018. In some of the nation's most watched and most generously funded contests Republicans narrowly retained the governorships in Florida and Georgia and Ted Cruz's Texas Senate seat. The GOP even eked out a victory in the Florida Senate contest where outgoing Governor Rick Scott knocked off three-term incumbent Bill Nelson. While Democrats came up short in statewide contests, they managed to pick off Republican-held congressional seats in every Growth State except North Carolina, where one seat remains unde- cided as of this writing. If the Democrat prevails in the 9th District, North Carolina will join the other Growth States that saw Democrats gain four Texas seats, three in Virginia, two seats in Florida, and one each in Georgia and South Carolina. Democrats made no headway in any of the Stagnant States.

Although not as clear-cut as Table 1.4, the timing of GOP domi- nance generally came earlier in Growth than Stagnant States. Table 1.5 shows when the GOP established itself as the majority in the legislative chambers and congressional delegations.[4] As reported in Table 1.5, Republicans established majorities in three Growth State chambers in the 1990s and by 2010 dominated all but three chambers, and in two of these (Virginia Senate and North Carolina House) had majorities for at least half a dozen years prior to 2010. In contrast, the earliest consistent majorities in the Stagnant States do not come until 2005, at which point, Republicans led seven Growth State cham- bers. Seven Stagnant State chambers did not come under GOP control before 2010.

Republicans established control of four Growth State congressional delegations but only two Stagnant State delegations before 2000. In three Stagnant States the GOP established itself in 2011 although it had led the Tennessee delegation for six years previously. In Texas the Tom DeLay (R)inspired mid-decade redistricting erased the last traces of Martin Frost's clever Democratic plan in 2005. North Carolina, where Republicans had led the delegation twice before for a total of ten years, has been under GOP control since 2013.

Table 1.5. Dates when GOP secured majorities in Southern state legislative delegations

	State Senate	State House	U.S. House
Growth States			
Florida	1995	1997	1989
Georgia	2003	2005	1995
North Carolina	2011	2011*	2013*
		(1995–1998, 2003–2004)	(1995–1996, 1999–2006)
South Carolina	2001	1995	1995*
			(1981–1982)
Texas	1997	2003	2005
Virginia	2015*	1999	1995–2019*
	(1999–2008)		(1971–1974, 1977–1986)
Stagnant States			
Alabama	2009	2011	1997*
			(1965–1966)
Arkansas	2013	2013	2011
Louisiana	2012	2010	1997
Mississippi	2011	2011	2011*
			(1997–1998)
Tennessee	2005*	2009	2011*
	(1995–1996)		(1993–1994, 1997–2002)

*Indicates that the GOP had a majority at some point before it established itself as the dominant party. The earlier periods of GOP control are shown in parentheses.

Source: Created by the author.

Republicans generally established control over Growth State Senates before Stagnant States; the earliest date of control in the latter comes in Tennessee in 2005 by which time the GOP was firmly in control of four Growth State Senates. Republicans have led two Growth State lower chambers since the 1990s and controlled three other states by 2005. The GOP took over the first Stagnant State lower house in 2009.

The Growth States in which Republicans made earlier gains have begun showing signs of a Democratic revival. As with other matters, the strength of the signs varies among the states with the least evidence coming from South Carolina, which on multiple dimensions is least like the other Growth States. The most pronounced erosion of GOP control has come in Virginia where Democrats control statewide offices, picked up three congressional seats in 2018 to secure a 7–4 advantage and came within one seat of organizing the lower chamber of the legislature following the 2017 elections. In contrast, Republicans have come into power in the Stagnant States only recently and the newness has not begun to wear off. Instead in some of these five states the Republican tide may have not yet crested. Consider, for example, the Tennessee legislature. While the state saw temporary GOP majorities in the past, only since 2005 in the Senate and 2009 in the House have Republicans consolidated their hold and now boast twenty-eight of thirty-three senators and seventy-four of ninety-nine representatives. As in other Stagnant States, Democrats are now at their lowest ebb and have few prospects for gain, other than the governorship, which rotates every eight years between the parties in Tennessee.

The in-migration to Growth States of not just Hispanics and Asians but also individuals from other parts of the country reduced GOP hegemony and contributed greatly to Barack Obama's 2008 Florida, Virginia, and North Carolina victories. The changing makeup of the population in terms of its ethnicity and where these individuals grew up has also pushed Georgia into the toss-up category in terms of presidential elections. In 2016 four Growth States were among the eleven most competitive states in the presidential election. The significance of these four is that they are among the six competitive states with the largest numbers of Electoral College votes. It is likely, therefore, that on into the next decade, and perhaps beyond, the key battlegrounds for the presidency will be the dynamic Southern states. Once the Hispanic population in Texas becomes sufficiently mobilized to put that state's electors into play, the South will have the potential to dominate close contests for the presidency.

In competing for the votes in these states, presidential candidates may have to temper their messages. Democrats may have to shift toward the center lest they lose too much of the Evangelical vote.

Republicans who have relied heavily upon the Evangelical vote may have to moderate their positions, as Evangelicals become a smaller share of an increasingly diverse electorate.

The South that Key saw as having a politics that focused on race is increasingly becoming one in which the most important differentiating factor is growth as the states of this region with expanding populations create new opportunities for Democrats to regain some of the positions that they held for the better part of a century. If, indeed, the growing states of the South become more competitive, the Republican Party whose ability to win the presidency in 2000, 2004, and 2016 and to secure congressional majorities hinged upon doing exceptionally well in the South may face the prospect of being largely shut out from the nation's highest office.

Growth in portions of the South has the potential to return the region's partisanship to something akin to what King knew although with the roles reversed. The states in which the GOP was making headway when King led the civil rights movement are now the states experiencing tentative shifts back toward the Democratic Party. The states that featured some of the most visible outbursts against efforts to promote equality remained loyal to the Democratic Party at least locally and fully embraced the GOP only later. In Alabama where the Montgomery Bus Boycott was one of the items birthing the civil rights movement, Mississippi where the Emmet Till lynching was another birthing element, and Arkansas where the first major violence surrounding school desegregation erupted at Little Rock's Central High, Democrats relinquished control of the legislatures only within the last decade. The echoes of the pact that bound the South to the Democratic Party in return for noninterference with racial practices for the better part of a century kept Republicans a minority in the Stagnant State's legislatures for an additional half century.

Plan of the Book

The chapters in this book explain how the South has fundamentally changed in the past half century and how that has dramatically altered national politics. Analyzing and explaining the transformation of U.S. politics since the explosive events of 1968 requires particular attention to the South. Indeed, a strong case can be made that the South has had the greatest impact on the transformation of U.S. politics and government. The last half century has witnessed the demise of the "sold (Democratic) South" and the rise of the Republican-dominated South, the rise of the largely Southern white Evangelical religious right movement, and vast demographic changes that have altered the political landscape of the region and national politics. Race remains important in understanding the region's politics, but as the Black Lives Matter Movement has reminded us, racial divisions and the conflict along that fault line are not unique to the South. Economic growth and accompanying population expansion are a major division in the region, with part of the South moving toward a dynamism that is the envy of the Rust Belt but also of Southern neighbors. Much as those lured from the North by the spread of air conditioning planted the seeds of a competitive GOP, today those attracted by the high-tech industries around Austin, North Carolina's Research Triangle, Atlanta's movie industry, the proximity of Washington to Northern Virginia, and Florida's beaches and retirement communities are breathing new life into the Democratic Party.

People and businesses continue to be drawn to the South by its favorable weather, racial/ethnic and age diversity, relatively low cost of living, an increasingly more educated workforce, and relatively inexpensive land. The continued social and economic diversification of the region has altered its politics and given rise to the "demographics is destiny" thesis.

Nothing has altered the South's politics more than the influx of racial/ethnic minorities. The region's nonwhite population has been on the rise since 1980. There has been an influx of minorities moving to the South from other parts of the United States (e.g., blacks leaving the North and returning home to the South, Puerto Ricans relocating from the Northeast, and in the wake of Hurricane Maria's devastation, from the island). Diversity in the country-of-origin of minorities moving to the South is often overlooked, yet critical to understanding a state's politics (e.g., Cubans versus Puerto Ricans in immigrant-rich Florida). The South's nonwhite population is younger than its white population. However, like the nation-at-large, the region's population is getting older as Baby Boomers turn sixty-five. Some states have aggressively recruited retirees from other parts of the country primarily for economic reasons. These newcomers have brought their party affiliations with them, often helping change a state's partisan mix. In Southern states with sizable senior *and* minority (younger) populations, there are more intergenerational political schisms, reflecting the intersection of race and age.

Chapter 2 examines the demographic changes of the South and their impact on national politics and government. The South has experienced explosive population growth over the past half century. States have grown at different rates; the highest rates of growth have been in Florida, Texas, Georgia, Virginia, and North and South Carolina. This sizable population influx has been largely driven by in-migration from Latin America, Asia, and other regions of the country (Midwest, Northeast).

The region's population growth has significantly increased its role in national politics. Southern states have gained thirty-one seats in the U.S. House of Representatives since 1950—a figure projected to increase yet again after the 2020 U.S. Census. A growing number of these congressional members are minorities and women—reflective of the region's changing demographics.

Chapter 3 describes and analyzes the national impact of the changing partisanship of the South. Indeed, nowhere has partisan change been as dramatic and as extensive as in the South. Half a century ago Republican electoral success rarely extended beyond presidential contests. Democrats had near total control of the region's public offices. Today the GOP is at or near its maximum strength in the region, except contests in Virginia where Democrats once again dominate statewide offices.

Across the last half century, the region and each of the states experienced a secular realignment. The time and pace of the change varied but generally began earlier in the Growth South than the Stagnant South. Today it is the South experiencing growth, and where the population is becoming more diverse, a swing back toward the Democratic Party has begun. Generally, the states in which Republicans first made gains are now at the forefront of those in which Democrats have started to rebound.

The South has experienced changes both in partisanship and its influence on the national scene. The region has lost some of its clout in Congress, but now often determines the winner in presidential elections, and Southern politicians can aspire to occupy the White House. The great strength registered by Republicans in the South has been essential to the ability of the GOP to organize Congress for most of the last generation.

No issue has defined the politics of the South more than race—the topic of Chapter 4. At the midpoint of the twentieth century, V.O. Key's (1949) classic work on Southern politics noted the centrality of race to all of the region's political landscape. He focused on impediments to black voting, but had nothing to say about black political activity in the region since it was nonexistent. Key's emphasis reflected the reality of a time when fewer than 10 percent of the region's African Americans could even vote.

The elimination of the infamous white primary shortly before Key published his volume and the phasing out of the poll tax precipitated a rise in African American voting, spurred in part by aggressive voter registration campaigns. By the late 1950s, about a quarter of the region's blacks had signed up to vote. By the time of the 1965 Voting Rights Act (VRA) black voter registration in the South had reached 43 percent. Two years after King's assassination, two-thirds of the region's eligible black adults had registered. Today, Southern African Americans vote at about the same rate as whites, and even higher in some recent presidential elections. The full participation of African Americans has been a major force in transforming the region's—and the nation's—politics.

The 1960s civil rights era completed the African American shift to near complete loyalty to the Democratic Party. Today the African American vote is the bulwark of the Democratic Party in the South. Republicans now dominate state legislative chambers in the region and governorships, leaving little policy influence for black or white Democrats in much of Southern state politics. The significantly growing minority populations in Southern states is making some of the region politically competitive, and, with strong African American support, the Democratic Party has made important inroads in Virginia, North Carolina, and Florida.

Chapter 5 examines the rise of the Evangelical, conservative-led religious right movement. In 1968 there was little discussion of the impact of the Evangelical vote. Neither national political party had ever
had the word "abortion" in its platform, and political observers barely
had anything to say about the role of religion in the national elections,
other than abiding concerns about how Michigan governor George
Romney's Mormon faith would affect his quest for the GOP presidential nomination. A half century later the dominant force in Republican
Party nominations in much of the South is the white Evangelical vote.
This transformation has had a profound impact on national politics.

The 1976 presidential campaign of native son Southerner Jimmy
Carter, an openly born-again Christian who spoke much about his
faith during the campaign, helped mobilize Southern Evangelicals.
Evangelicals in the region had been largely absent from the political
scene, with such leaders as the Rev. Jerry Falwell advocating that they
keep their distance from "matters of this world" such as the political
sphere to allow God to work His will on earth. But with Carter's campaign, many Southern Evangelicals developed the habit of political
participation, and that presented a challenge to Republicans who had
long advocated a "Southern strategy" of appealing to mostly Southern
white voters since the era of civil rights.

Evangelical discontent with Carter's policies created an opening for
the GOP, and some conservative leaders successfully reached out to
Falwell and other faith leaders to help mobilize Evangelicals into the
Republican Party. Presidential candidate Ronald Reagan campaigned
for Evangelical votes in the South, even commencing his national
campaign in Mississippi. Positions he staked out favored pro-life,
school prayer, and tax benefits for private religious schools.

The shifting of the Evangelical vote in the South to become over
time the foundation of Republican Party support has consequences
on the partisan equation in the region and nationally as well. The once
"solid South," meant solidly Democratic. By the 1980s it had become
the nearly solid Republican South in presidential elections. As the
Republicans increasingly took the South, the Democrats have tried to
make up for their losses in Southern white votes by building a coalition of minorities in the Northeast, Midwest, and West Coast.

The 2016 presidential election of Donald J. Trump confounded political observers, although the GOP nominee's strong showing in the South did not. Chapter 6 examines how white racial resentment in particular helped Trump overcome many political liabilities that would easily have sunk the candidacies of other presidential aspirants in Southern states. The racial resentment worked differently in the primary and the general election.

Trump won every primary held in the South, with the exception of Texas, which had a favorite son candidate in Senator Ted Cruz. The South was Trump's strongest region in terms of statewide victory, although not in percentage of the electorate. Data analysis suggests that Trump's racial rhetoric and attitudes found a receptive audience in the South, especially among GOP primary voters. In the general election, Trump's "Make America Great Again" campaign, his anti-immigration positions, and his fierce rejection of Black Lives Matter and affirmative action, may have given his campaign a slight advantage in the white South (compared to white voters in the rest of the nation), although this seems indistinguishable from the support that prior Republicans have received from that demographic in recent elections. In that sense, Trump's showing was the culmination of a long-standing trend of Southern white voting in national elections. Trump's remarkable embrace of racist tropes such as "Obama was born in Kenya," "blacks have it better than whites today," and "Black Lives Matter is a terrorist organization," affected white voting patterns nationwide. His popularity in the South shows that that region found something special in Trump, something beyond what GOP voters found in other regions. While we cannot say that was a uniquely Southern response to Trump's racist posturing, or some sort of Southern affinity for a white backlash to a Second Reconstruction, we can observe that the South, which went strongly for George Wallace in 1968 and Barry Goldwater in 1964, at least did not find these statements disqualifying. Indeed, Southern whites strongly embraced Trump in the primaries and in the general election.

Trump's success with racial rhetoric shows the Southernization of the Republican Party. After all, he triumphed unexpectedly in a number of non-Southern states, most memorably Wisconsin, Pennsylvania, and Michigan. He did so by doing better than expected among less educated whites and a decline in black turnout as compared to the 2008 and 2012 Barack Obama elections. Perhaps racial resentment as a way of motivating white voting, which explained so well Wallace's surge in the South in 1968, is now a nationwide phenomenon whose Southern origin is barely remembered, like key lime pie or Waffle Houses.

The chapters that follow thus describe and analyze the key variables of Southern political change of the past half century that have transformed the national political landscape. It is impossible to comprehend the fundamental changes in U.S. politics and government without examining their Southern roots.

2

The Changing Demographics of the South and Its Impact on National Politics*

The South of 2018 is vastly different than it was fifty years ago.[1] The major reason is the region's explosive population growth, which has, in turn, elevated its clout on the national political stage, most notably in presidential and congressional elections. Former governors Bill Clinton of Arkansas (1993–2001) and George W. Bush of Texas (2001–2009) both served two terms as president, for example, and U.S. Senator Marco Rubio (R-Florida), remains a potential presidential candidate despite his failed run in 2016.

Going further back to 1960, Southern states have gained thirty-two seats in the U.S. House of Representatives—a figure projected to increase yet again after the 2020 U.S. Census. A growing number of these members of Congress are minorities and women.

The region's growing clout reflects major *changes in its electorate*, underscoring the importance of examining the link between demographics and politics, especially in high-growth areas. Once viewed as a "conservative monolith," the South's political leanings have become more "nuanced—and moderate" (Seitz-Wald 2018) with the "imported" politics of newcomers of all ages, races and ethnicities, and occupations.

In 1968, whites and blacks were the predominant racial groups across the whole region (with few exceptions), and most lived in the state in which they were born. But this biracial makeup has changed

---

* Anthony Cilluffo is co-author of this chapter.

with the in-migration of Hispanics and Asians, and the rise of multiracial populations (Livingston 2017; Taylor and Pew Research Center 2016). The lines between racial and ethnic groups have become blurred by higher rates of intermarriage and the growing number of persons with mixed ancestry (Perez and Hirschman 2009). Adding to the diversity has been the influx of domestic migrants—young professionals flocking to Southern cities for job opportunities and retirees moving south for the quality of life and lower cost of living.

Over the fifty-year period covered by this book, the most common factors associated with the region's population explosion have been economic growth and jobs, immigration (particularly of Hispanics and Asians), in-migration from other states, improvements in the educational attainment of residents, rising incomes, and the quality of life (recreational opportunities and mild weather). The region's population growth has occurred in tandem with the diversification of its economy (Kotkin 2013), although state-by-state differences are discernible.

The major focus of this chapter is on the roles that immigration and economic growth and diversification have played in transforming the American South. Other chapters provide more in-depth analyses of how specific demographic shifts have changed politics and electoral successes directly related to race, party, and religion.

Nation's Fastest Growing Region

Behind the remarkable transformation of the South has been its significant population growth. The South (defined as the eleven states of the old Confederacy) has grown more in the past fifty years than any other region in the United States (see Table 2.1). Between 1970 and 2010, Florida (+177 percent), Texas (+125 percent), and Georgia (+111 percent) have seen the most explosive growth, followed by North Carolina (+88 percent), South Carolina (+79 percent), and Virginia (+72 percent). This book calls these six states the Growth States. Together, the population of the Growth

Table 2.1. Population change in Southern states, 1970–2010

	1970 population	2010 population	Percent change, 1970–2010
Growth States			
Florida	6,791,418	18,801,310	177 percent
Texas	11,198,655	25,145,561	125 percent
Georgia	4,587,930	9,687,653	111 percent
North Carolina	5,084,411	9,535,483	88 percent
South Carolina	2,590,713	4,625,364	79 percent
Virginia	4,651,448	8,001,024	72 percent
U.S. Overall	203,302,031	308,745,538	52 percent
Stagnant States			
Tennessee	3,926,018	6,346,105	62 percent
Arkansas	1,923,322	2,915,918	52 percent
Alabama	3,444,354	4,779,736	39 percent
Mississippi	2,216,994	2,967,297	34 percent
Louisiana	3,644,637	4,533,372	24 percent

Source: Table 12. Population: 1970–2010 in U.S. Census Bureau. 2012. "United States Summary: 2010 Population and Housing Unit Counts." *2010 Census of Population and Housing*. September 2012.

States more than doubled (+117 percent) over the period. Slower, though positive, rates of growth have occurred in Tennessee (+62 percent), Arkansas (+52 percent), Alabama (+39 percent), Mississippi (+34 percent), and Louisiana (+24 percent). The population of these five Stagnant States increased just 42 percent in the past fifty years.

What separates the fortunes of the Growth and Stagnant States? In large part, it is economic and social dynamism. The states that have attracted a diverse group—in race and ethnicity, age, and socioeconomics—of in-migrants (domestic and international) have experienced the highest rates of population growth. These factors are explored in greater detail later in this chapter.

Nothing has altered the South's politics more than the increase in the numbers of racial and ethnic minorities and the changing composition of the nonwhite population. In 1970, the South was about three-quarters non-Hispanic white and 20 percent black. Together, these two racial and ethnic groups made up 94 percent of the population. But even this fact understates the monolithically black-and-white nature of the 1970s South. In that year, only Texas and Florida had sizable minority populations that were not black (predominantly Hispanic). In each of the other states of the South, *98 percent or higher of the population was either white or black.*

The New South looks much different. In 2017, 55 percent of the population was non-Hispanic white. *A higher share of the South's population is Hispanic (20 percent) than non-Hispanic black (19 percent).* Although the South's Hispanic population continues to be most significant in Texas and Florida, the Hispanic population grew in all Southern states. Only Mississippi and Alabama have populations that are less than 5 percent Hispanic. Here, again, the difference between Growth and Stagnant States is clear. In Growth States, 52 percent of the population is white, 23 percent Hispanic, 18 percent black, and 4 percent Asian. In Stagnant States, 66 percent of the population is white, 25 percent black, 5 percent Hispanic, and 2 percent Asian.[1]

The region's nonwhite population, largely foreign-born, has been on the rise since 1980. This demographic shift has been driven largely by international migration (Latin America, Asia). But there has also been an influx of minorities moving to the South from other parts of the United States (e.g., blacks leaving the North and returning home to the South, Puerto Ricans moving south from northeastern states such as New York and New Jersey). *Demographers project that racial minorities will also be the "primary demographic engine" of future growth, "countering an aging, slow-growing and soon to be declining white population"* (Frey 2018a).

Migration: International and Domestic

Before 1965, immigrants coming to the United States had been largely European. But amendments to the Immigration and

Nationality Act in 1965 eliminated a national quota system and prioritized skilled workers and family reunification (Tienda and Sánchez 2013). These revisions drew more Hispanics and Asians (male and female) to the United States and the South in the 1970s, giving rise to the region's economic growth spurt (Basu 2015; Pew Research Center 2015).

International migration has been an important driver of racial, ethnic, and economic change across the South. The foreign-born share of the population has increased in all the Southern states since 1970 (see Figure 2.1). Four states—Florida (21 percent), Texas (17 percent), Virginia (13 percent) and Georgia (10 percent)—have the largest foreign-born populations. Big metropolitan areas such as Houston, Dallas, Nashville, Charlotte, Atlanta, Raleigh, and Orlando

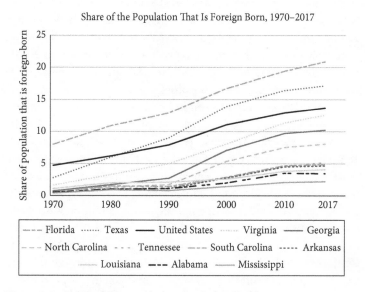

Figure 2.1. Share of the population that is foreign born, 1970–2017

Source: Data for 1970 through 2000 from Gibson and Jung (2006), Table 14. Nativity of the Population for Regions, Divisions, and States: 1850–2000. Data for 2010 and 2017 from 2010 and 2017 American Community Survey 1-year estimates, Table B05012 Nativity in the United States.

have become immigrant magnets, with growth rates highest in these metros' suburban ring communities (Kotkin 2013).

Foreign-born immigrants come for different reasons: to escape oppression or a collapsing economy in their native country, for a better education, as part of a family unit, or as recruits to fill specific jobs in the United States. These differing paths into the country led to divergent outcomes once settled: those escaping oppression tend to have lower educational and skill levels and have lower incomes and higher poverty rates, while those who enter the country to take a high-skilled job (such as H-1B visa holders) typically have higher incomes than the average American.

The heavy influx of foreign-born residents understates the overall impact of immigrants. The share of the foreign-born population across the South increased between 1994 and 2017 from 7 percent to 14 percent. But so, too, did the share of second-generation immigrants—those born in the United States to at least one foreign-born parent—from 6 percent to 10 percent.[2] Research shows that second and third generations are less hamstrung by language inadequacies and more likely to register and vote (Trevelyan 2016). (First-generation immigrants are often hampered by citizenship requirements, among other difficulties.)

Since 2010, *net domestic migration* (those moving in, minus those moving out) has exceeded net international migration in six states: Florida, Georgia, North Carolina, South Carolina, Tennessee, and Texas (see Figure 2.2). (Three other states had more residents move out than move in domestically: Louisiana, Mississippi, and Virginia.) Florida and Texas are particularly strong magnets for domestic migrants—over 1 million more have moved to those states than moved out—because they are attractive to migrants from states beyond the South, in particular, New York, California, and Illinois. These two states have more large metropolitan areas offering greater employment opportunities for newcomers than more rural states such as Mississippi and Louisiana.

Because those who move tend to have greater resources or—in the case of younger professionals—employment prospects, gaining a large number of residents from other states can quicken the pace of

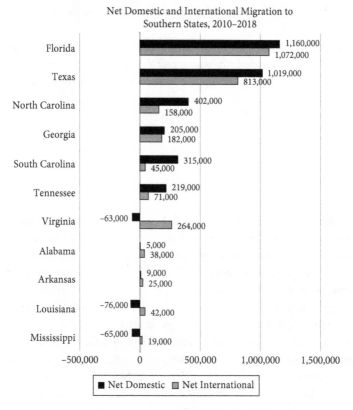

Figure 2.2. Net domestic and international migration to Southern states, 2010–2018

Note: All numbers rounded to nearest thousand. Net migration measures the difference between the number of people moving in minus those moving out. In Florida, for example, about 1.2 million more people moved in than moved out domestically, while in Mississippi, 65,000 more people moved out of the state than moved in domestically.

Source: U.S. Census Bureau vintage 2018 population estimates, Table 4. Cumulative Estimates of the Components of Resident Population Change for the United States, Regions, States, and Puerto Rico: April 1, 2010 to July 1, 2018.

economic, geographic, and demographic transformation. Conversely, losing a large number of relatively better-off residents can make it harder for the states that are already behind on socioeconomic indicators to catch up with other states.

Diversity within Immigrant Groups

Focusing exclusively on broad racial and ethnic groups rather than on differences related to country-of-origin can yield misleading conclusions. When analyzing the link between immigration-related growth and political change, one must dig deeper into the socioeconomic and political differences within each group.

Hispanics

The influx of Hispanics has changed the populations of most Southern states and their politics. For example, Mexicans—who are generally less likely to naturalize as citizens and therefore be eligible to vote (López, Bialik, and Radford 2018)—are a majority of the Hispanic population of every Southern state except Florida, Louisiana, and Virginia (see Table 2.2). Cubans, a plurality of Florida Hispanics, are one of the few minority groups to lean Republican. However, younger Cubans who are less interested in anti-Castro politics are leaning more Democratic. (Anti-despotic sentiments have occasionally prompted immigrants from Venezuela, Nicaragua, and Colombia to vote Republican, but not consistently.) In Virginia, there are about as many Salvadorans as Mexicans.

In all Southern states, Puerto Ricans are the second or third most common national origin for Hispanics. Unique among Hispanic origin groups, Puerto Ricans are already U.S. citizens when they migrate to the mainland and can therefore immediately register to vote. Reasons for the immigration of Puerto Ricans include the economic recession gripping the island and the devastation caused by Hurricanes Irma and Maria. After arriving, many Puerto Ricans have settled in the area around Orlando, Florida.

Historically, fewer Hispanic immigrants have come via Central or South America (López, Bialik, and Radford 2018) than from Mexico or Cuba (Tienda and Sánchez 2013). Florida, however, is now home to many immigrants from Colombia, the Dominican Republic, Venezuela, Nicaragua, and Honduras. Virginia's sizable Salvadoran

Table 2.2. Detailed origin among Southern Hispanics, 2017
(Numbers are percent of the state's Hispanic population)

	1	2	3	4	5
Alabama	Mexican	Guatemalan	Puerto Rican	Honduran	Cuban
	58	12	11	2	2
Arkansas	Mexican	Salvadoran	Puerto Rican	Guatemalan	Spaniard
	74	11	3	2	2
Florida	Cuban	Puerto Rican	Mexican	Colombian	Dominican
	28	21	14	7	5
Georgia	Mexican	Puerto Rican	Guatemalan	Salvadoran	Cuban
	56	10	7	5	4
Louisiana	Mexican	Honduran	Puerto Rican	Cuban	Salvadoran
	37	20	7	6	5
Mississippi	Mexican	Puerto Rican	Guatemalan	Cuban	Dominican
	64	8	4	4	3
North Carolina	Mexican	Puerto Rican	Salvadoran	Honduran	Colombian
	57	11	6	5	3
South Carolina	Mexican	Puerto Rican	Colombian	Guatemalan	Honduran
	53	14	6	4	4
Tennessee	Mexican	Puerto Rican	Salvadoran	Guatemalan	Honduran
	61	9	6	5	4
Texas	Mexican	Salvadoran	Puerto Rican	Honduran	Guatemalan
	86	3	2	1	1
Virginia	Salvadoran	Mexican	Puerto Rican	Guatemalan	Honduran
	23	23	12	7	6

Source: Author's analysis based on U.S. Census Bureau, Table B03001 Hispanic or Latino Origin by Specific Origin, 2017 American Community Survey 1-year estimates.

population and Louisiana's Honduran population are other notable exceptions.

Since the Great Recession began in 2007, there has been an increase in immigrants from three Central American nations—El Salvador, Guatemala, and Honduras—known as the Northern Triangle (Cohn, Passel, and Gonzalez-Barrera 2017). Besides seeking better economic opportunities and reunification with family and friends already in the

United States, many have migrated to the South to "[escape] conflict, generalized violence and targeted persecution" (Holmes 2018). The "unrelenting turmoil" in the Northern Triangle has driven many to flee with their children (Gamboa, Atencio, and Gutierrez 2018).

Immigrants from these areas continue to have less education and lower incomes than other immigrants (Rosenblum and Brick 2011). Fewer become naturalized citizens. Relatively high shares are undocumented, sometimes giving rise to anti-immigrant sentiments among legal residents, especially when the immigrants are perceived as working for lower wages and taking jobs from natives (Rosenblum and Brick 2011).

Blacks

Among the nation's black population, immigrants form a rising share. The largest concentrations come from the Caribbean and Africa (Anderson and López 2018). In Southern states, black immigrants are most prevalent in Florida. In Miami, for example, one in three black residents is an immigrant, mostly from the Caribbean (Ordoñez 2015). Foreign-born blacks from the Caribbean (Haiti, Jamaica, and Trinidad and Tobago) often differ politically from U.S.-born blacks. In south Florida, for example, Caribbean and U.S.-born blacks increasingly run against each other for state and local offices (MacManus 2017: 13–15, 27–28). By party, Caribbean-American blacks lean Democratic but less solidly so than U.S.-born blacks.

The return of many Southern-born blacks to the South was responsible for black population growth beginning in the 1970s (Kopf 2016). For the first half of the twentieth century, African Americans fled the former Confederate states for their personal safety, to escape institutional racism, and in search of jobs. The pattern slowly began to reverse itself in the 1970s. Blacks gradually migrated back to the South because of deteriorating economic conditions in many cities in the Northeast and Midwest, the growth of jobs in the New South, the lower cost of living, strong long-standing family and kinship ties there, and improved race relations in the region (Kotkin 2015).

The 2000 U.S. Census registered the first increase in the region's black population in more than a century. Since 2000, black population growth has been highest in Atlanta (deemed the "unofficial capital of black America"), and in the Raleigh, Charlotte, Orlando, Miami, Richmond, San Antonio, Austin, Houston, and Dallas-Fort Worth metro areas, including their suburbs (Kotkin 2015).

Asians

Nationally, Asia has replaced Latin America as the biggest source of new immigrants—a trend that is projected to continue (Cohn and Caumont 2016). The largest shares of Asian groups in the United States are (in descending order) Chinese, Indian, Filipino, Vietnamese, Korean, and Japanese (López, Ruiz, and Patten 2017), although this varies by state (see Table 2.3). Asian Indians, for example, form at least a quarter of the Asian population in six Southern states (Florida, Georgia, North Carolina, Tennessee, Texas, and Virginia).

Diversity in the Asian American community is remarkable. Socially, some groups, such as the Chinese and Japanese, have a long history in this country. Others, such as the Vietnamese, came in the 1970s wave of immigration following changes in U.S. immigration law and the end of the Vietnam War. Other groups are still more recent arrivals. Economically, a higher incidence of Asian immigrants arrives via green cards based on employer sponsorship, reflecting their higher educational levels and highly sought technological skills (Pew Research Center 2015).

Not all Asians arrive for high-paying jobs. Other origin groups, such as Hmong and Bhutanese, are more likely to arrive as refugees and have low educational attainment, low income, and high rates of poverty.

Regionally, between 2000 and 2010, the *increase* in Asian American residents was highest in the South, especially in Georgia, North Carolina, and Virginia, although proportionately they make up a relatively small percent of the total population. Many locate in metropolitan area suburbs, reflecting "ideas of entrepreneurship, the primacy

Table 2.3. Detailed origin among Southern Asians, 2013–2017 (Numbers are percent of the state's Asian population)

	1	2	3	4	5
Alabama	Chinese	Asian Indian	Korean	Vietnamese	Filipino
	20	19	19	15	9
Arkansas	Asian Indian	Chinese	Vietnamese	Laotian	Filipino
	24	17	14	11	10
Florida	Asian Indian	Filipino	Chinese	Vietnamese	Korean
	28	18	17	13	5
Georgia	Asian Indian	Chinese	Korean	Vietnamese	Filipino
	34	14	14	14	6
Louisiana	Vietnamese	Asian Indian	Chinese	Filipino	Korean
	41	14	14	10	5
Mississippi	Vietnamese	Asian Indian	Chinese	Filipino	Korean
	24	21	17	15	7
North Carolina	Asian Indian	Chinese	Vietnamese	Filipino	Korean
	32	16	13	8	7
South Carolina	Asian Indian	Chinese	Filipino	Vietnamese	Korean
	23	21	16	10	9
Tennessee	Asian Indian	Chinese	Filipino	Vietnamese	Korean
	26	17	11	11	10
Texas	Asian Indian	Vietnamese	Chinese	Filipino	Pakistani
	29	20	15	10	6
Virginia	Asian Indian	Filipino	Chinese	Korean	Vietnamese
	25	14	14	14	12

Source: Author's analysis based on U.S. Census Bureau, Table B02015 Asian Alone by Selected Groups, 2017 American Community Survey 5-year estimates.

of family in society and the importance of education" (Fouriezos 2018; see also Fuchs 2018).

As with Hispanics, cultural and political differences exist among different groups of Asians. The Asian vote is "hardly monolithic, divided both by age and cultural background" (Fouriezos 2018). Historically, a higher proportion of Asians than other minorities registered as independents and were swing voters, often supporting Republican presidential candidates. But that has changed; Asian voters now lean Democratic, although less solidly than blacks. Most of the Asian newcomers to the South have been described as "transplants from liberal states on the coasts" who are "chasing economic opportunity and a cheaper cost of living" (Grovum 2014).

Migration and Residential Patterns Vary by Age, Generation

Like the nation at large, the region's population has gotten older as Baby Boomers turn sixty-five. The "graying of America has left a distinctive geographical fingerprint" (Rogerson 2018). States with larger-than-national-average shares of senior residents are Florida, South Carolina, Arkansas, Alabama, Tennessee, and North Carolina. For years, older retirees, mostly white, moved to Florida to enjoy their elder years. Many still do, but others, including some Floridians, have chosen more amenity-laden retirement communities in mountainous parts of Georgia, North Carolina, and Tennessee as their retirement destinations (McWhirter 2018; Rogerson 2018).

These older newcomers, mostly white, migrating to the South have brought their party affiliations with them, occasionally changing the partisan mix of a state or locality. However, they, like younger in-migrants, increasingly have chosen to retire in areas with economically and politically like-minded residents (Cook 2015; The Economist 2008). In Florida, for example, a huge retirement community near Ocala (The Villages) is largely Republican-voting, while many south Florida retirement communities have large concentrations of Democrats. Regardless of their partisan leanings, older voters are high-turnout voters.

In contrast, the South's nonwhite population is younger than its white population. Among the large nonwhite populations, the multiracial population is the youngest, followed by Hispanics, blacks, and Asians (Gao 2016). While older in-migrants tend to live in smaller, more rural and suburban areas, the younger, more racially and ethnically diverse, migrants more often move to cities such as Atlanta, Charlotte, Nashville, and Austin. Such areas are popular destinations for younger adults, many of whom are well-educated professionals, drawn by job opportunities and more youth-oriented local cultural scenes. College towns, ports, and coastal areas are also magnets, such as Columbia in South Carolina; Jacksonville in Florida; and Newport News, Norfolk, and Virginia Beach, in Virginia (Miller 2018).

Young adult millennials, considerably more racially/ethnically diverse than boomers (Cohn and Caumont 2016; Frey 2014), are much more likely than their elders to hold liberal views on many political and social issues. Politically, they are *less likely to identify with either major political party*. Their turnout rates are generally lower than older citizens, especially in midterm elections. However, more are running for elected office, particularly young women—a higher proportion of whom are college educated—and women of color (Talbot 2018). Southern states with sizable senior *and* minority (younger) populations have more intergenerational political schisms, reflecting the intersection of race and age, and clashes over the widening generational income gap.

Economic Growth and Diversification

People and businesses continue to be drawn to the region from other parts of the United States and foreign countries because of job opportunities and/or the relatively lower cost of living, and more affordable housing. "Migration is changing the [national] economic center of gravity to the South" (Moore 2015).

Following national trends, the economic base (the largest industry by employment) in the South has shifted from agriculture (1950s) to manufacturing (1960s–1970s) to professional, educational, and healthcare services (2000 and later). (See Table 2.4.) Retail trade, construction, and transportation, communications, and utilities industries have consistently been important sources of employment. Since 1970, the transition away from manufacturing toward employment in professional, educational, and healthcare industries has been swift across all Southern states. In 1970 manufacturing was the largest industry in every Southern state except Florida and Louisiana. In 2017 it was only the third largest in several states, and even smaller in

Table 2.4. Largest industries of employment by state, 1970–2017 (Number are percent of the state's civilian household employed population ages sixteen and older)

	1970	1990	2017
All	Manufacturing	Professional, education, healthcare	Professional, education, healthcare
	22	22	28
	Professional, education, healthcare	Manufacturing	Retail trade
	16	18	19
	Retail trade	Retail trade	Manufacturing
	16	17	10
Alabama	Manufacturing	Manufacturing	Professional, education, healthcare
	27	23	28
	Professional, education, healthcare	Professional, education, healthcare	Retail trade
	15	22	18
	Retail trade	Retail trade	Manufacturing
	15	16	15
Arkansas	Manufacturing	Manufacturing	Professional, education, healthcare
	24	22	29
	Professional, education, healthcare	Professional, education, healthcare	Retail trade
	17	21	19
	Retail trade	Retail trade	Manufacturing
	15	17	14

(*continued*)

Table 2.4. Continued

	1970	1990	2017
Florida	Retail trade	Professional, education, healthcare	Professional, education, healthcare
	19	21	27
	Professional, education, healthcare	Retail trade	Retail trade
	17	20	20
	Manufacturing	Manufacturing	Business and repair
	14	11	8
Georgia	Manufacturing	Professional, education, healthcare	Professional, education, healthcare
	25	20	27
	Professional, education, healthcare	Manufacturing	Retail trade
	15	19	19
	Retail trade	Retail trade	Manufacturing
	15	17	11
Louisiana	Professional, education, healthcare	Professional, education, healthcare	Professional, education, healthcare
	17	26	30
	Retail trade	Retail trade	Retail trade
	17	17	19
	Manufacturing	Manufacturing	Construction
	16	12	8
Mississippi	Manufacturing	Manufacturing	Professional, education, healthcare
	27	24	29
	Professional, education, healthcare	Professional, education, healthcare	Retail trade
	17	22	18
	Retail trade	Retail trade	Manufacturing
	15	16	14

Table 2.4. Continued

	1970	1990	2017
North Carolina	Manufacturing	Manufacturing	Professional, education, healthcare
	34	27	29
	Professional, education, healthcare	Professional, education, healthcare	Retail trade
	14	20	19
	Retail trade	Retail trade	Manufacturing
	14	16	13
South Carolina	Manufacturing	Manufacturing	Professional, education, healthcare
	29	26	28
	Professional, education, healthcare	Professional, education, healthcare	Retail trade
	15	19	20
	Retail trade	Retail trade	Manufacturing
	14	16	14
Tennessee	Manufacturing	Manufacturing	Professional, education, healthcare
	31	24	29
	Professional, education, healthcare	Professional, education, healthcare	Retail trade
	16	20	19
	Retail trade	Retail trade	Manufacturing
	14	16	13
Texas	Manufacturing	Professional, education, healthcare	Professional, education, healthcare
	19	22	27
	Retail trade	Retail trade	Retail trade
	17	18	18
	Professional, education, healthcare	Manufacturing	Construction
	17	14	9

(continued)

Table 2.4. Continued

	1970	1990	2017
Virginia	Manufacturing	Professional, education, healthcare	Professional, education, healthcare
	19	23	32
	Professional, education, healthcare	Retail trade	Retail trade
	18	16	16
	Retail trade	Manufacturing	Public administration
	15	15	9

Note: This analysis uses the IND1990 harmonized variable made available through IPUMS-USA. See Ruggles et al. (2018) for additional information.

Source: Author's analysis of IPUMS microdata 1970 decennial census 1 percent metro form 1, 1990 decennial census 1 percent, and 2017 American Community Survey (Ruggles et al. 2018).

others. Instead, *professional, education, and healthcare industries are the largest employer in every Southern state.*

Changes have also occurred in the occupations of Southerners. Since 1970, the shares of workers have nearly doubled in two occupational segments: (1) professional or technical occupations, and (2) managerial, official, and proprietor occupations (see Table 2.5). The shares of workers in farm, crafts, and operator (such as bus and truck drivers) occupations have all fallen. But differences emerged on the basis of race. Compared with whites, a sharper decline took place in the share of blacks employed in farm, service, and labor occupations. Conversely, blacks experienced larger gains in their shares employed in clerical and sales occupations. Additionally, while the share of whites employed in managerial roles roughly doubled (from 10 percent to 18 percent), it increased ten times among blacks (from 1 percent to 10 percent).

Changes in the socioeconomic makeup of the population have accompanied these trends. When the economy was largely agricultural, median family incomes were low. But as low-skill farm jobs gave way to middle- and high-skill jobs, family incomes have been rising.

Table 2.5. Largest occupations for whites and blacks, 1970–2017
(Numbers are percent of the state's civilian household employed population ages 16 and older)

Occupational groups	All			White			Black		
	1970	1990	2017	1970	1990	2017	1970	1990	2017
Professional/technical	14	19	25	16	21	29	8	13	20
Service workers	13	13	16	8	10	12	32	23	22
Managers, officials, proprietors	8	13	15	10	15	18	1	5	10
Clerical	17	18	15	19	18	14	7	17	18
Operators	18	13	9	16	11	7	23	20	13
Craftsmen	14	11	8	15	12	8	9	8	6
Sales	8	7	6	9	8	7	2	3	5
Laborers	5	5	4	3	4	3	12	8	5
Farmers	3	1	1	3	1	1	6	1	0

Note: Numbers may not sum to 100 percent due to rounding. This analysis uses the OCC1950 harmonized variable made available through IPUMS-USA. See Ruggles et al. (2018) for additional information.

Source: Author's analysis of IPUMS microdata 1970 decennial census 1 percent metro form 1, 1990 decennial census 1 percent, and 2017 American Community Survey (Ruggles et al. 2018).

The educational attainment of the population has followed a similar path, increasing over time. These economic changes have also impacted the geographic distribution of the population, with increasing shares of the population concentrating in larger urban areas where the best job opportunities are.

Some economists say it is difficult to generalize about growth in specific sectors because of the "heterogeneity of economic activity throughout the region" (Diment, Masterson, and Ulama 2016). But they have concluded its economy "has diversified into knowledge-based industries in advanced manufacturing, technology, finance and energy . . . [and] is notable for its established transport network and energy infrastructure, as well as competitive rates for land and labor costs and an attractive business climate."

The continued social and economic diversification of the region has altered its politics and given rise to the "demographics is destiny" thesis. Economic growth has been strongest in the South's fast-growing metropolitan areas with younger, minority populations that are more liberal in their politics. Demographer Joel Kotkin (2013) attributes the fading of the old Confederacy's (conservative) political banner to "demographic trends, economic growth patterns, state business climates, flows of foreign investment and, finally and most surprisingly, a shift of educated workers and immigrants to an archipelago of fast-growing urban centers."

These economic changes have also transformed the geography of the region. A higher share of the population was living in an urban area in 2010 than in 1970 in all eleven Southern states. In North Carolina, South Carolina, Georgia, Virginia, and Florida, urbanization occurred faster than in the nation overall. Texas, a Growth State that already had a relatively high share of the population living in an urban area in 1970, remains one of the most urbanized Southern states.

Among the nation's one hundred largest metropolitan areas, some of the biggest population gains have been in Dallas, Houston, Atlanta, Orlando, Austin, Tampa, and Miami. Fast-growing smaller interior metro areas are Knoxville and Memphis in Tennessee and Little Rock in Arkansas (Frey 2018b). Indeed, in

1950, no Southern city was counted among the ten largest metro areas in the country. By 1980, two Southern cities (Dallas-#8 and Houston-#9) were on the list. By 2017, four of the ten largest metro areas were in the South (Dallas-#4, Houston-#5, Miami-#7, Atlanta-#9).

Companies are drawn to the South by its labor force, quality of life, and generally pro-business tax climate. Of the eleven states in the South, only Mississippi and South Carolina do not have at least one S&P 500 company headquartered in their state. The list of companies headquartered in the South includes some of the most recognizable ones in the world, including Walmart (Bentonville, Arkansas), Coca-Cola (Atlanta, Georgia), Exxon Mobil (Irving, Texas), and Bank of America (Charlotte, North Carolina). While some companies are "native" to the South, others relocate their headquarters there. In 2016 alone, Atlanta attracted significant relocations from Mercedes-Benz USA, NCR, Honeywell, and General Electric (Copenhaver 2016).

Additional qualities and amenities draw in-migrants to Southern cities besides the high-value companies operating there. Some Southern cities are known for their cultural and entertainment offerings, including Nashville, Tennessee; Austin, Texas; and Miami, Florida. Beaches, mountains, the Appalachian Trail, and parks are draws for the recreationally inclined. The South is also home to several highly competitive college football teams and numerous professional sports teams. The diversity of Southern cities is appealing to younger migrants, as well.

Higher Levels of Education and Rising Income: Gender and Race Differences

For many years, the educational level of Southerners lagged considerably behind the nation at large, as did wages. As the region has grown, the gap has narrowed. Rising educational and income levels are attributable to better schooling among "home state" residents and to the in-migration of generally more well-off people from other regions.

Educational attainment, measured by the share of the population twenty-five and older with at least a bachelor's degree, continues to rise in all Southern states, although only Virginia has a higher share than the United States overall (see Figure 2.3). In lockstep with this trend, median family income has risen in all eleven Southern states.

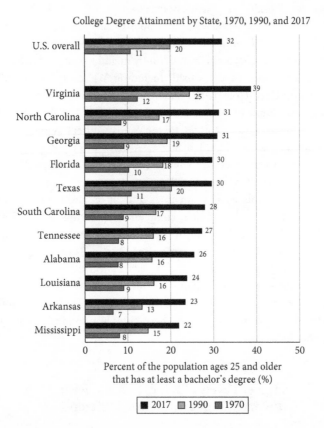

College Degree Attainment by State, 1970, 1990, and 2017

Percent of the population ages 25 and older
that has at least a bachelor's degree (%)

■ 2017 ▨ 1990 ▨ 1970

Figure 2.3. College degree attainment by state, 1970, 1990, and 2017
Note: Based on population ages twenty-five and older.

Source: Data for 1970 and 1990 from U.S. Census Bureau, *Census 2000 PHC-T-41. A Half-Century of Learning: Historical Statistics on Educational Attainment in the United States, 1940–2000,* Table 6a. Percent of the Total Population 25 Years and Over with a Bachelor's Degree or Higher by Sex, For the United States, Regions, and States: 1940–2000. Data for 2017 from 2017 American Community Survey 1-year estimates, Table S1501 Educational Attainment.

Aggregate figures mask some major class differences *between* racial and ethnic groups, but also *within* different racial and ethnic groups. Many who have been left behind are minorities. Fewer blacks and Hispanics than whites are going to college, and fewer have the finances needed to secure middle-class jobs at a time when "minorities make up nearly half of American youth; and . . . will [soon] account for all the growth in the U.S. workforce" (Frey 2017).

Black and Hispanic families earn less than white families in all Southern states, as well as the country overall (see Figure 2.4). However, the extent of racial income inequality varies. In Louisiana, the median black family earns less than half of what the median white family in the state earns, and black families in Mississippi, South Carolina, and Alabama also experience income inequality higher than the national average. With the exception of South Carolina, these are all Stagnant States. However, among the two other Stagnant States, Arkansas has black-white family income inequality a little lower than the country overall, and Tennessee has the lowest inequality of all Southern states. In Tennessee the median black family earns 70 percent of what the median white family earns.

The typical Hispanic family earns more than the typical black family in five Southern states (Virginia, Florida, Louisiana, South Carolina, and Mississippi), about the same in Arkansas, and less in the other five. White-Hispanic income inequality is highest in Alabama, where Hispanic families earn half of what white families do. It is higher than the nation overall in North Carolina, Texas, Louisiana, and Georgia. It is lowest in Florida, where the median family income for Hispanics is 69 percent of what it is for whites.

The reasons for these racial and ethnic difference are long-rooted and complex. Differences in educational attainment and employment play a significant role (Johnson and Neal 1998). Inequalities in local public school funding, access to financial services, and a higher share of single-parent (overwhelmingly female) households are also important. Entrenched racism and discrimination (Bertrand and Mullainathan 2004) and incarceration rates also influence the observed inequality. These factors combine to reduce economic mobility of racial minorities (Chetty et al. 2014).

Others point to the shortage of adult Southerners, particularly persons of color, with education or training beyond high school

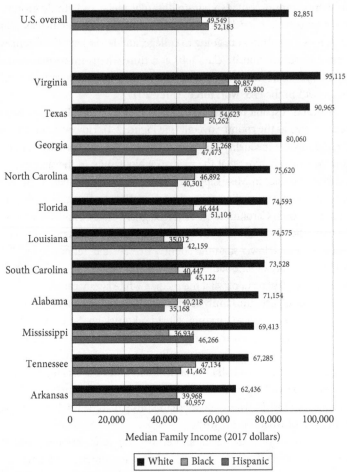

Median Family Income in Past 12 Months by Race and Ethnicity

	White	Black	Hispanic
U.S. overall	82,851	49,549	52,183
Virginia	95,115	59,857	63,800
Texas	90,965	54,623	50,262
Georgia	80,060	51,268	47,473
North Carolina	75,620	46,892	40,301
Florida	74,593	46,444	51,104
Louisiana	74,575	35,012	42,159
South Carolina	73,528	40,447	45,122
Alabama	71,154	40,218	35,168
Mississippi	69,413	36,934	46,266
Tennessee	67,285	47,134	41,462
Arkansas	62,436	39,968	40,957

Median Family Income (2017 dollars)

■ White ▨ Black ■ Hispanic

Figure 2.4. Median family income in past twelve months by race and ethnicity

Note: All dollar amounts are in 2017 inflation-adjusted dollars. Whites and blacks are single-race non-Hispanics. Hispanics are of any race.

Source: U.S. Census Bureau 2017 American Community Survey 1-year estimates (Tables B19113B, B19113H, B19113I).

to fill middle-skill jobs that do not require a four-year college degree (Johnson 2018). States with lagging growth rates, such as Mississippi and Louisiana, have lower educational attainment rates and larger minority populations, placing more pressure on elected officials at the state and federal levels to spend more on vocational training.

Regardless of race or ethnicity, more women than men go to college. The gender gap is widest among Hispanics (13 percent), blacks (12 percent), and whites (10 percent) and narrowest among Asians (3 percent) (Lopez and Gonzalez-Barrera 2014). Since 1982, women have been awarded a majority of U.S. college degrees (Perry 2017). This educational advantage has contributed to higher voter-turnout rates among women than men, wider gender gaps in vote patterns within each racial/ethnic group, and more women running for political office. More broadly, differences in voter educational attainment—those with bachelor's and advanced degrees versus those without—have widened, leading some to conclude that "the new cultural divide is education" (Zitner and DeBarros 2018).

Demographic Shifts Yield More Polarized Electorates

The importance of examining the link between demographic shifts and the changing politics of the South is clear. In the fifty years since the civil rights movement and Martin Luther King Jr.'s assassination, population growth, largely driven by international and domestic migration, has made the South's politics more polarized, with sharp differences by race, place of birth, age, education, income, and gender:

> Democrats rely on a "Coalition of Transformation," built around minorities, millennials, and socially-liberal, college-educated whites (especially women) largely comfortable with this social and racial transformation; Republicans mobilize a competing "Coalition of Restoration" that revolves around the older, blue-collar, rural, and

religiously-devout whites most uneasy with some or all of these changes (Brownstein 2015).

While most Southern states have voted heavily Republican in recent presidential elections, some states—those with the highest shares of minorities, international and domestic in-migrants, and higher growth rates (Florida, Virginia, Georgia, North Carolina, and even Texas)—have become more competitive from a partisan perspective and more racially/ethnically and gender diverse in whom they elect to national, state, and local offices.

Over the past fifty years, the South's changing racial/ethnic demographics have propelled more blacks (see chapter 4) and Hispanics to the U.S. Congress. Blacks have been elected to the U.S. Senate from Mississippi and South Carolina and to the U.S. House from every Southern state but Arkansas. Hispanics have been elected to the U.S. Senate and the U.S. House from Texas and Florida. Moreover, one Asian (a female Vietnamese-American Democrat) has been elected to the U.S. House from Florida.

Women from the South have made big strides in getting elected to Congress, reflective of their rising educational attainment levels and, more recently, the influence of #BlackLivesMatter and #MeToo movements. According to statistics generated by the Center for American Women in Politics (2018b), just three Southern women were in the U.S. House in 1977. By 2018, seventeen women were in that chamber—six from Florida; three from Texas; two each from Alabama, North Carolina, and Tennessee; and one each from Georgia and Virginia. Florida's delegation was by far the most diverse—two black Democrats, one Cuban Republican, one Vietnamese Democrat, and two white Democrats. In the Senate, two states—Mississippi and Tennessee—elected females, both white Republicans. The increased presence of women in Congress is changing how things are done: "Women get more bills passed, their bills have more cosponsorships than their male counterparts, women in general are more progressive" (Alter 2018).

All but four southern states (Alabama, Arkansas, Tennessee, and Mississippi) have elected nonwhites to a statewide office (president,

U.S. Senate, governor, other nonjudicial offices) (Ballentine 2016). Southern women of color have served as a governor (Indian American Republican from South Carolina) and lieutenant governors (African American Republican, Florida; Cuban American Republican, Florida). A white female was elected governor by Alabamans. She had previously been elected lieutenant governor (Center for American Women and Politics 2018a).

Black women have been elected to the state legislatures of all Southern states except Arkansas, Latinas to the Florida, Georgia, Tennessee, Texas, and Virginia legislatures (Center for American Women and Politics 2018c). Women of color have been elected mayor in Atlanta, New Orleans, and Charlotte—three of the nation's one hundred largest cities. Minority candidates (female and male) have enjoyed more success in local elections in areas with large numbers of black, Hispanic, or Asian residents. The number of those racially/ethnically diverse areas is on the upswing as the South's demographic composition continually changes in response to population growth and economic diversification.

Looking Forward

Demographically, the South of 2018 looks little like it did fifty years earlier. Rapid population growth has led to increasing racial and ethnic diversity. People of all ages are moving into the South, although to different places and for different reasons, helping to remake the socioeconomic composition of the region. These changes have played out during a period of realignment in regional and national politics, in which Republicans have expanded their regional dominance in presidential elections to victories at the state and local level. But continued in-migration, accompanied by economic diversification and racial/ethnic and generational shifts, is beginning to push the political pendulum in the opposite direction.

This changing of political direction is largely being driven by the region's Growth States, characterized by their significant increases in jobs and wage levels, higher rates of domestic and international in-migration, increasingly more racially/ethnically and age diverse populations, and more representative (race/ethnicity, age, gender) governing bodies. In contrast, the Republican hold on the Stagnant States remains strong, reflecting the markedly different demographic and socioeconomic composition of their electorate.

Throughout the region, economic changes have produced different political geographies even within the same state—a pattern observable nationally as well. The resurgence of a Southern economy centered in middle- and high-skill occupations has created a patchwork of highly educated, relatively well-off cities surrounded by less-educated and relatively worse-off rural areas. Increasingly, statewide elections are won or lost in the suburbs of the large metro areas, where these two worlds collide. Another regional political dynamic is the growing conflict between Democrat-controlled city governments and Republican-controlled state governments. This same dynamic (geographically based partisan preference differences) has resulted in more partisan splits within Southern state congressional delegations.

Looking ahead, several big questions remain. Chief among them: *Is demographics destiny?* If so, the long-term changes remaking the South will create headwinds that will blow against Republican dominance in the region. As noted, some of the states at the forefront of these demographic changes have already become the nation's premier battlegrounds in presidential elections.

What about intergenerational conflicts? Retirees are migrating to Southern states in large numbers. While these recent movers tend to be relatively well-off financially and healthy, they will exert greater strain on public services in their new states as they age. This will place greater demands on younger residents to support them. And generational replacement will put younger politicians with different values and economic views in charge.

As racial and ethnic diversity increases, *what role will identity politics play in an increasingly polarized political environment?* Will overtures to race and ethnicity as get-out-the-vote (GOTV) strategies be as effective as the region's population gradually becomes more multiracial?

Finally, *how will the two major political parties react to increasing shares of voters shunning both parties,* especially younger voters and certain minority groups (Hispanics, Asians)?

What *is* certain is that the South has, and will continue, to play a major role in the nation's politics. It remains the best vantage point for observing the political consequences of major demographic and socioeconomic changes.

3

The Changing Partisanship
of the South and Its Impact
on National Politics

While no region's politics have remained static, partisan loyalties in the South have changed more dramatically over the last half century than in any other part of the nation. In the late 1960s many parts of the South remained as committed to the Democratic Party, at least to offices below that of the president, as they had been for the previous century. Today and for the last quarter century, the South has provided the strongest support for the GOP and has been the mainstay of the Republican's ability to organize Congress. In this chapter, we examine how the region has changed from the nation's most reliably Democratic area to the bedrock of conservative Republicanism.

One-Party Democratic South

The period of largely unchallenged Democratic hegemony in the South exceeds the length of numerous governmental systems. The life of the Soviet Union, the rule of the house of Stuart in Britain, and the independence of all the former colonies that separated after World War II are less than the era of Democratic dominance in the South, which extended for almost a century following the end of Reconstruction. To cite but a few examples of the pervasiveness of Democratic control: from 1880 to 1952 there were 188 opportunities for the GOP to win a Southern state's Electoral College votes. In only six of these did the GOP succeed as Herbert Hoover carried five Rim South States in 1928 and Tennessee voted for Warren Harding in 1920. The Seventeenth Amendment ended the indirect election of senators, putting the choice in the hands of the public. The first popularly elected Republican senator from the South took office in 1961 when John Tower (TX) won the special election to fill the seat vacated when Lyndon B, Johnson became vice president. Louisiana did not elect a Republican senator until 2004. Excluding Tennessee, which always had a Republican base in the Smokey Mountains, the South's first Republican governors of the twentieth century took office in 1967 in Arkansas and Florida. Georgia became the last state to put a Republican at the governor's desk when Sonny Perdue ended fifty consecutive elections won by Democrats who led the state from 1873 to 2003. From 1933 to 1953, the South had more than one hundred members in the U.S. House. During those two decades the only Republicans represented the two easternmost Tennessee districts.

During the century when Democrats controlled Southern states' politics they were barred from the nation's highest office. After Tennessee's James Knox Polk left the White House in 1849 no Southern politician won the presidency until Lyndon B. Johnson in 1964.[1] Southern politicians, regardless of their skill, were ineligible to lead the nation because of their and their region's stands on race. Richard Russell (D-GA) was the acknowledged leader of the Senate from the late 1940s on through the 1950s and 1960s (White 1956). In both 1948 and 1952 he sought the Democratic nomination as president but was never viewed as anything more than a regional candidate despite his widely admired political skills and subject matter expertise. He was Lyndon B. Johnson's mentor and presidents as diverse as John Kennedy and Richard Nixon recognized Russell as the model senator whom new members should study and emulate. Many at the time would have agreed with President Harry Truman's assessment that had Russell come from any other region, he would have become president (Shaffer 1980).

Not only did the South not provide presidents, the region infrequently took a hand in the selection of the chief executive. With Republicans occupying the White House for all but four terms from the Civil War until the Great Depression, electors from the solid Democratic South often stood almost alone when registering their preferences. Only in 1884 and 1916 were Southern electors critical in the choice of the president.

Banished from the presidency, Southern politicians concentrated their efforts in Congress. From 1891 to 1961 all but two of the Democrats who served as Speakers of the House came from the South and one of the exceptions, Champ Clark (1911–1919), came from the Border State of Missouri. Southerners who played oversized roles in the Senate included Georgia's Walter George (1922–1957) and Richard Russell (1933–1971), Texans Tom Connally (1929–1953) and Lyndon B. Johnson (1949–1960), Virginia's Harry Byrd (1933–1966) and Arkansas's Joseph Robinson (1913–1937) and William Fulbright (1945–1974). The old bulls who ruled the Senate as the Citadel described by William White (1956) came from the South. From 1920 when Oscar Underwood (AL) was chosen to lead Senate Democrats until 1961, the party had a Southern leader for twenty-five years.

Beginning with the onset of the New Deal, Southerners usually constituted a minority of the Democratic membership in Congress. They magnified their influence through the committee leadership posts obtained through seniority and by finding allies with whom to fashion a floor majority. With the solidification of the seniority norm as the basis for selecting committee chairs, Southerners filled a disproportionate share of these posts during the era when chairs had few checks on their power. The committees ruled over by Southerners often were among the most powerful, for example, Appropriations, Ways and Means and Finance, Armed Services, and House Rules. It was in Congress, as one wit observed, that the South exacted revenge for Appomattox.

The Southerners, most of whom were conservative on a range of issues beginning with the end of World War II (Sinclair 1982), forged an informal, but prolonged alliance with Republicans. Dubbed the Conservative Coalition, when Southern Democrats and Republicans linked arms they usually won floor votes. From 1939 to 1956, the Conservative Coalition succeeded on more than 90 percent of the House roll calls on which it mobilized (Brady and Bullock 1980). During its heyday the Conservative Coalition appeared on 20–25 percent of the roll calls and in some Congresses won every time it mobilized. Figure 3.1 shows that through the 1980s and 1990s the

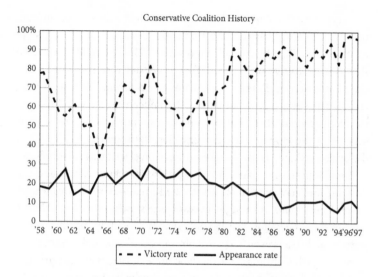

Figure 3.1. Conservative Coalition history

Source: Stephen Gettinger, "R.I.P. to a Conservative Force," *CQ Weekly* (January 9, 1999), 82.

Conservative Coalition continued to prevail more than 80 percent of the time. However as conservative Southern Democrats were replaced by conservative Republicans or more moderate Democrats, the frequency of the Coalition's appearances decreased and during the last decade that Congressional Quarterly tracked its activities it appeared on only about a tenth of the roll calls.

Republican Emergence

The modern Republican Party in the South scored its first successes during the Eisenhower era. In 1952, the retired general won four of the six Rim South states.[2] It is also during his presidency that the first Republicans in the century won House elections in Florida and Texas and re-established enclaves in western North Carolina and Virginia.

The first Republican rustlings in the Deep South come in the next decade in the guise of Barry Goldwater (Cosman 1966). Not only did he sweep these five states but his coattails produced the first Republican members of Congress in almost a century. Georgia and Mississippi each sent one Republican to Congress in 1964 while Alabama elected Republicans to five of its seats. The Goldwater candidacy produced the South's second Republican senator when Strom Thurmond (SC) changed parties. It also brought a Republican South Carolinian to the House when Albert Watson, who had supported Goldwater while serving in the House as a Democrat, lost his seniority as a result of disloyalty, resigned from Congress, then won election as a Republican.

The Eisenhower years and the Goldwater candidacy made the Republican Party respectable first in the Rim South and a decade later in the Deep South. Although success came slowly, more Republicans appeared on the ballot. In 1950 only twenty-five of the Southern congressional districts even had a Republican candidate, and nine of these were in North Carolina. During the course of the 1950s, the greatest number of districts with a Republican candidate was forty-four in 1956 as individuals hoped to catch a ride on Eisenhower's re-election coattails.[3] In 1964, Republicans contested seventy-three districts and won fifteen. [4] In the immediate wake of the Goldwater candidacy, twenty-seven additional Republicans won seats in the Georgia legislature and the South Carolina Senate welcomed its first six Republicans.

The drift toward the GOP took multiple detours. Of the states that voted for Goldwater, only South Carolina backed Richard Nixon in 1968. The other Deep South states along with Arkansas rallied to the independent candidacy of Alabama governor George Wallace running on a platform that promised to reverse the Johnson administration's civil rights initiatives. Nixon swept all of the other Rim South states except for Texas, which Johnson managed to hold for his vice president Hubert Humphrey.

In 1972, the South joined the rest of the nation in rejecting George McGovern and re-electing Nixon in a landslide. This marked the first election in which the entire South rallied to a Republican presidential candidate. Nixon's coattails swept an additional fifty-two Republicans to the region's state legislatures and increased the number in the congressional delegation from twenty-seven to thirty-four.

But as Nixon's landslide turned into the Watergate mudslide, the chief executive was not the only victim. The 1974 mid-term erased the congressional gains of 1972 and as Nixon left the White House he was followed by eighty-two Republicans turned out of Southern legislative chambers. The number of Republican Southern legislators bottomed out two years later when Jimmy Carter enjoyed the greatest success of any Democratic presidential nominee since Roosevelt carried the region in 1944. Carter failed to replicate FDR's feat but did win every state but Virginia. The back-to-back events of Watergate and the Carter election temporarily stopped GOP expansion.

Regional pride no doubt played a role in Carter's 1976 victory as he became the first president from a Deep South state. Four years later he had alienated so many whites that he retained only his home state as Ronald Reagan ended the Georgian's political career. The Reagan years marked the high-water point in Republican presidential success in the South. In the three presidential elections of the 1980s the only Democratic victory came in Georgia in 1980. In the other thirty-two state contests, the Democratic nominee often failed to attract 40 percent of the vote. It was during the 1980s that the white conservative vote finished its secular realignment to the GOP soon to be followed by many white moderates (Black and Black, 2002).

After rarely being a player in presidential elections in the century after the Civil War, the region can no longer be ignored. The winner of the White House would have remained a private citizen in 1960, 1976, 2000, 2004, and 2016 had he done no better in the South than in the rest of the nation. And while the region's electors were not essential to winning the presidency in other years, the South now usually votes for the winner. In ten of the fifteen elections beginning with 1960, most Southern states have voted for the president. In an eleventh election, five states backed Nixon in 1968, only Texas supported Democrat Hubert Humphrey and five states supported George Wallace. In the twenty-one presidential elections between 1876 and 1956 most Southern states supported the winner nine times.

When the South unites behind a presidential candidate, as it did in 1972, 1984, 1988, 2004, and 2008 its choice is well on the way to rounding up the 270 electors that secure the keys to the White House. With the South's current strength in the Electoral College, should a candidate win all eleven states, it would be necessary to get slightly less than 30 percent of the electors in the rest of the nation to become president. In 2016 when all the South but Virginia voted for Trump, Clinton needed 68 percent of the non-Southern electors—a challenge that proved impossible.

The South has achieved near or total unanimity in the Electoral College in eight of the dozen presidential elections beginning with 1972. Nonetheless, several states are now judged swing states, which places them among the ten or twelve that receive the overwhelming share of the campaign budgets and candidate visits. Florida with its dozens of electors leads the list where it is joined by North Carolina. Virginia was a swing state in both Obama elections but in 2016 Republicans largely conceded it to Clinton. Georgia, which gave Trump a five-point victory, will have swing state status in 2020.

Not only is the South a player in determining the outcome of a presidential contest, after being excluded from the Oval Office from 1849 until 1963, Southern politicians now have a shot at becoming president. In the thirty-two years between 1977 and 2009, Southerners held the nation's highest office for all but the eight years of the Reagan presidency.

Reagan's initial election also coincided with Republicans regaining the strength they had in Southern legislatures prior to Watergate as their seat total exceeded three hundred for the first time. Six years later the ranks of Republican legislators crossed the four hundred threshold. Reagan's coattails helped Republicans win U.S. Senate seats in Alabama, Florida, and North Carolina while in Georgia, Mack Mattingly ran ahead of Reagan to become Georgia's first popularly elected Republican senator. With the election of Paul Trible (VA) in 1982, the GOP briefly held half the South's Senate seats before Democrats mounted a comeback.

Another manifestation of secular or gradual realignment is visible in the results of state legislative and congressional elections. As shown in Figure 3.2, the gradual increase in GOP office holding finally reaches and maintains a majority of both chambers of Congress following the 1994 wave election. And although Democrats continued to claim a majority of the South's state legislative seats, the 1994 wave witnessed the GOP winning majorities in the North and South Carolina Houses and the Florida and Tennessee Senates. Two years later, when Republicans

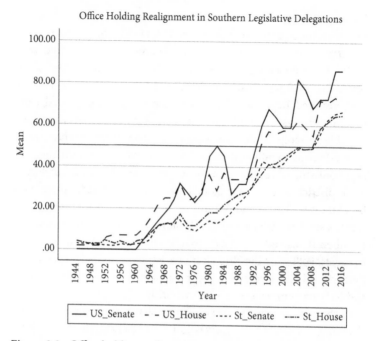

Figure 3.2. Office holding realignment in Southern legislative delegations

added four seats in the Florida House, the Sunshine State became the first in the region in which the GOP controlled both chambers. When Jeb Bush won the governorship in 1998, the GOP secured unified control of its first Southern state, which it has maintained. As shown in Figure 3.2, after 2008, Republicans hold most of the seats in the upper and lower legislative chambers of Southern states.

The GOP continued to make gains in the new century. In 2005 when David Vitter went to the Senate, Louisiana became the last Southern state to elect a Republican. Sonny Perdue's upset victory in 2002 gave Georgia its first GOP governor in 130 years as it became the last Southern state to have a Republican chief executive (Bullock 2003). In 2009 Republicans could boast of majorities in most (twelve of twenty-two) Southern legislative chambers. Six years later every Southern legislative chamber was in Republican hands, as shown in

Figure 3.3. Except for Virginia, as will be discussed later, Democratic prospects for securing legislative majorities in the short run are poor.

After securing a majority of the Southern congressional seats in 1995, Republican growth stalled at less than three-fifths of the seats. The 2010 wave election dethroned Speaker Nancy Pelosi (D-CA), restored Republican control of the House, and yielded gains of hundreds of state legislative seats across the nation. In the South, Republican ranks in the U.S. House increased from seventy-two to ninety-four as Republicans added seats in every Southern state except Louisiana where they already held every seat except the majority-black district. Republicans gained four seats in Florida; three each in Tennessee, Texas, and Virginia; and a pair each in some of the region's smallest delegations of Alabama, Arkansas, and Mississippi. Republicans also added an Arkansas Senate seat and 150 state legislative seats. Following the 2016 elections, Republicans had 86 percent of the region's U.S. Senate seats, 72 percent of the U.S. House delegations, and 66 percent of the state legislative offices.

In the early 1950s, the overwhelming share of the white Southern electorate considered themselves to be Democrats. The Eisenhower

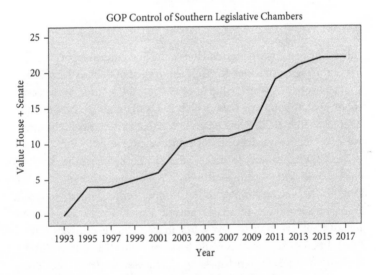

Figure 3.3. GOP control of Southern legislative chambers

campaigns made it acceptable to be a Republican. Previously, only transplanted Yankees and a few oddballs would admit to favoring the GOP, so pervasive was the Democratic Party, which controlled virtually every political office save in the region's mountainous areas. But with the Republican ticket headed by a distinguished general and almost a century after the Civil War one could acknowledge favoring the GOP. The infusion of Northerners lured to the South by job opportunities provided talented leadership to the emerging party (Bullock and Kanso 2015). Initial converts to the GOP came chiefly from the ranks of the most conservative Democrats. The departure of these individuals from the right wing of the party resulted in the median Democratic voter shifting leftward. This in turn made the Democratic electorate more tolerant of moderates and to the extent that the party nominated centrists, still more conservative Democrats became uncomfortable and decamped to the GOP, leaving the bulk of the remaining Democrats still less conservative. The departure to the GOP invariably involved whites.[5] With the enforcement of the VRA, which by 1970 had succeeded in rooting out the remaining legal barriers to African-American participation, decreases in the ranks of white Democrats meant that blacks constituted a larger share of the party.

When the Democrats succeeded in retaining many statewide offices on into the 1990s, it was thought that the winning electoral combination was strong support among African Americans coupled with at least 40 percent of the white vote (Black and Black 2002). Democratic presidential nominees after Carter could not reach the white vote threshold but many gubernatorial and senatorial candidates did. Today, at least in the Deep South where minority populations are more numerous, a rule of thumb is that to win statewide offices a Democrat needs for African Americans turnout to constitute 30 percent of all voters coupled with getting about 30 percent of the white vote. That is the combination that sent Doug Jones to the Senate in the 2017 Alabama special election. African Americans continue to cast about 90 percent of their votes for Democrats.

The Democratic electorate is now heavily African American. Florida and Louisiana have partisan registration and ask voters to indicate their race or ethnicity when signing up to vote. A review of the registration figures for those states shows that Louisiana Democrats in 2018 are 56 percent African American while 94 percent of Republicans are white. Among voters eligible to vote in the 2016 general election in Florida, 83 percent of Republicans were white while 29 percent of Democrats were black. Florida has one of the smallest black populations in the South. Another way to look at the partisanship of African Americans is that 81 percent of this group registered as Democrats and only 3.5 percent registered as Republicans.[6] On the Republican side, registrants are overwhelmingly white, except in Florida where there is a history of Cuban Americans identifying with the GOP because of the stands it has taken on the Castro regime.

Georgia also asks registrants to indicate their race or ethnicity, but the state has open primaries so voters need not make a choice of party when they register. After each election, Georgia's secretary of state does an audit of participation and reports the numbers of voters in the Democratic and Republican primaries by race. Figure 3.4 shows that in the early 1990s, African Americans cast less than a quarter of the vote in Democratic primaries. During most of the 2000s, the black share of the Democratic primary vote remained slightly below half. But in 2010 blacks accounted for 58 percent of the Democratic primary vote. The black share rose to almost two-thirds in 2014 before slipping to 62 percent in 2016 and 60 percent in 2018, with almost a third of the vote coming from whites. On the Republican side, whites have consistently cast more than 92 percent of the primary vote. At the same time that blacks first outnumbered whites in the Democratic primary, most Georgians began voting in the Republican primary.

In general elections, the best source of information on voting preferences by race comes from exit polls. In 2008, when all Southern states were polled, Barack Obama's share of the white vote ranged from 11 to 42 percent with a median of 26 percent (Bullock 2010). This was about the same as what John Kerry attracted in 2004. The 2000 election when the presidency was open and thus a good comparison with 2008 and 2016 had exit polls that saw the white vote for Al Gore range from 17 to 43 percent with a median of 26 percent. In 2016, six Southern states had exit polls. Hillary Clinton's share of the white vote ranged from 21 to 35 percent with a median of 29 percent. Three states in which whites have least frequently backed Democratic presidential

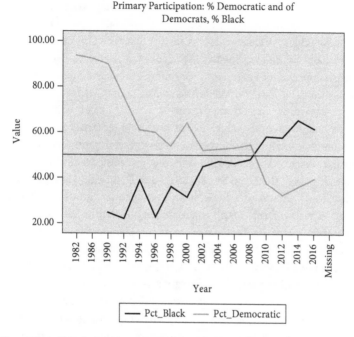

Figure 3.4. Primary participation: percent Democratic and of Democrats, percent black

nominees, Alabama, Louisiana, and Mississippi, were excluded from the 2016 exit poll. Had all Southern states been sampled in 2016, the median white support for Clinton would probably be lower than for the states included in the sample. One indication of how poorly Clinton fared among white, rural voters in a Deep South state is provided by almost entirely white Georgia counties where Clinton's vote had to come from whites. In some of these she managed less than 10 percent. In 2012, Obama got more than 10 percent of the vote in each of these overwhelmingly white counties.

As black voters have come to dominate Democratic primaries more African Americans have secured nominations for statewide offices. In 2014 five of the Democrats nominated for statewide posts in Georgia were black women. When Democrats were still the dominant party,

Georgia elected African Americans as attorney general (twice), and labor commissioner (three times). In 2002 Texas Democrats nominated an African American for the Senate.[7] African Americans have been nominated for the U.S. Senate in Alabama, Georgia and Mississippi and for governor in Virginia, Georgia, and South Carolina. The Virginian, Douglas Wilder, remains the only African American elected governor in a Southern state.

Of the thirty-nine congressional seats held by Democrats in 2017 whites had only one-third. The largest racial grouping, African Americans, filled twenty of the seats and were joined by five Hispanics and an Asian. The Deep South's last white Democrat, Georgia's John Barrow, fell victim to a Republican gerrymander in 2014. Arkansas joins the five Deep South states having no white Democrats in Congress. Only in Tennessee are most Democratic members of Congress (two of two) white. The largest concentration of white Democrats (five) comes from Florida and Texas had three as of 2018.[8] No other Southern state had more than two.

A racial transformation is also well underway in Democratic ranks in Southern state legislatures. The Democratic delegations in fourteen of the twenty-two Southern legislative chambers were predominantly black in 2018. In Florida and Texas the bulk of the Democratic legislators are nonwhite, and in Texas Hispanics outnumber African Americans by a large margin. Only in Arkansas and Virginia do whites dominate the ranks of Democratic legislators. The latter state is well on its way to turning blue while the Arkansas chambers were among the last to go Republican, not shifting in party control until 2013. Republicans may make additional gains in the Razorback State and that might result in its Democratic caucus becoming predominantly black. Figure 3.5 shows how the number of Democratic seats in the lower chambers of Southern legislatures has fallen by more than half over the last fifty years. The number of the Democratic seats now held by African Americans has risen from zero in 1962 to more than 260 and exceeds the ranks of whites. In every state except Virginia the numbers of white senators is in single digits. Georgia, which with fifty-six has the region's largest senate has eighteen Democrats, only four of whom are white. The largest white Democratic House delegations number in the low twenties.

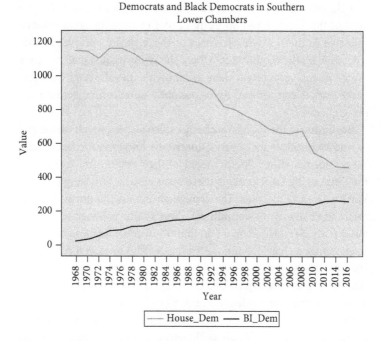

Figure 3.5. Democrats and black Democrats in Southern lower chambers

The South and the Contemporary Congress

As the South has become more significant in presidential elections and often the home of the chief executive, its influence in Congress has weakened. Southern power began to wane even when Democrats controlled Congress. During the 1950s the House Rules Committee occupied a strategic point in the South's defense against progressive policies. On this, the smallest House committee, Southern Democrats led by arch-conservative chairman Howard "Judge" Smith (D-VA) could join with Republicans to keep liberal legislation approved by substantive committees off the floor. This ended in 1961 when by the narrowest of margins the House expanded the Rules Committee from twelve to fifteen and liberals secured an 8–7 majority (Hardeman and Bacon 1987). In time, appointments to Rules became the purview of the Speaker and Minority Leader making the committee responsive to the policy preferences of the majority party leadership. Also unlike other committees where the seniority norm allows committee members to retain their assignments into the next Congress, party leaders can remove Rules members should they betray party preferences.

Beginning in the 1970s, Southerners also learned that if they hoped to lead committees they must demonstrate loyalty to the Democratic Party's agenda. Three Southerners lost their committee chairs when the Democratic Caucus made those posts elective following the post-Watergate wave election. The change abrogated the norm that had awarded chairs to the committee's most senior member of the majority party. Seniority remains an important consideration, but ceases to guarantee a chair. Having waited for decades to chair a committee, conservative Southern Democrats came to embrace more moderate stands so as to be acceptable to the Democratic Caucus's liberal majority. Taking more moderate stands in order to satisfy the demands of the Democratic leadership often made these legislators vulnerable to attacks from Republican challengers. Alabama senator Richard Shelby, one of several conservative Democrats who switched to the GOP, spoke for many when he explained, "I do not believe that there is any future for a conservative Southern Democrat I the Democratic Party. . . They're marginalized, they're being used . . ." (Black and Black 2002, 370).

The leadership of the Democratic Party had long included at least one moderate Southerner. The party tradition saw a progression with the party whip advancing to become party leader and then, during the decades when Democrats controlled the House, ultimately becoming Speaker. The path by which Southern moderates such as Sam Rayburn and Jim Wright advanced to the speakership was closed off when the first step toward becoming Speaker, service as whip, became elective. For years, the whip was an appointed position, and the selection for that post alternated between a moderate Southerner and a moderate Northerner (Nelson 1978). But after it became an elective office in 1986, no moderate Southerner has entered the leadership ranks.[9] The only Southerner to join the

Democratic leadership team in the last three decades, James Clyburn (SC), is left of center.

Not only have Southern moderates not advanced in the party hierarchy, their influence in the caucus and on the floor has weakened as their numbers declined. For decades beginning in the 1940s, much of what Congress produced was fashioned by the Conservative Coalition, an informal arrangement in which Southern Democrats joined with Republicans and outvoted Northern Democrats (Brady and Bullock 1981; Manley 1973; Shelley 1983). Over time Southerners inclined to side with Republicans against their fellow Democrats decreased, either replaced by Republicans or Democrats in the party's mainstream (Black and Black 2002). The last effort of moderates to rein in the more liberal members of the caucus came in the guise of the Blue Dogs who took their name from the feeling that they were being choked until they turned blue by their party's liberal leadership. Unlike the Boll Weevils of the heyday of the Conservative Coalition who were exclusively from the South or Border States, southerners in the Blue Dog ranks were augmented by Democrats from around the country. They had some success in slowing the Democratic leadership in the 111th Congress (Jones 2009) but when the 2010 wave election swept away many of their members they ceased to play a critical role.

The demise of Southern Democrats as a force in Congress has been partially offset by a greater importance of Southern Republicans. To understand the role of the South in the GOP dominance of the House for most of the last quarter century requires some background. After World War II but when Republicans had few if any seats in the South, the GOP won majorities of the non-Southern House seats from 1946 through 1968 except for 1958 and 1964 as shown in Figure 3.6. Nonetheless due to their abysmal showing in the South, Republicans managed to take control of the chamber only in 1947–1948 and 1953–1954. Now the geographic bases of the parties have reversed. Without the solid GOP majorities in the South, Democrats would have reclaimed control of the House in 1996 and retained it for all but one term. Figure 3.7 shows that Republicans could have held on to the Senate a bit longer after the 1994 coup but Democrats would not have needed Jim Jeffords's (VT) switch midway through 2001 to organize the Senate. And if partisan strength in the Senate were the same in

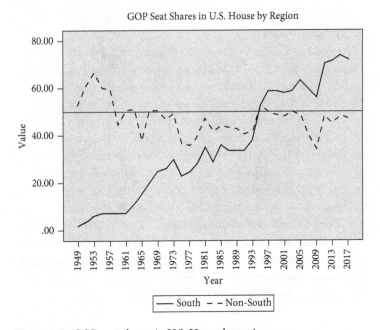

Figure 3.6. GOP seat shares in U.S. House by region

the South as elsewhere, Democrats would have dominated the upper chamber beginning in 2005. As of 2017, the South provided 38 percent of the GOP Senate seats, well above the region's 22 percent share of the chamber, and 41 percent of the GOP House delegation, about ten points more than the region's share of the House. If Republicans retain their current strength in Congress, Democrats have to win 62 percent of the remaining Senate seats and 60 percent of the House in the rest of the country to achieve majority status.

Not only was success in the South critical to the shift in party control since the middle of the 1990s, the region supplied much of the early leadership. The GOP House hierarchy immediately after the 1995 takeover consisted of a Southern triumvirate. The architect of the triumph, Newt Gingrich (GA), served as Speaker and was joined by Majority Leader Dick Armey (TX) and Minority Whip Tom DeLay (TX). The Midwest has supplied Republican House speakers since Gingrich's resignation in 1998. Currently the only Southerner among

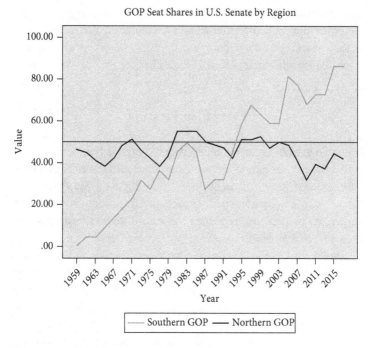

Figure 3.7. GOP seat shares in U.S. Senate by region

GOP House leaders is Whip Steve Scalise (R-LA). In the Senate, Trent Lott (MS) became majority whip when Republicans organized the Senate in 1994 and advanced to majority leader in 1996 when Bob Dole (KN) resigned to devote full time to his bid for the presidency. Lott was succeeded by Bill Frist (TN), so Southerners led the Senate for a decade save for the eighteen months of the 51–49 Democratic majority after Jeffords (VT) switched parties in 2001. Since Frist retired, Mitch McConnell (KY) has led the GOP with his understudy twice being from the South—Lott for 2007 and John Cornyn (TX) from 2013 to the present. No Senate Democrat has held a leadership post since Ted Kennedy (MA) supplanted Russell Long (LA) as whip in 1969.

The Southern wing of the GOP has provided some of its most conservative members and they have pulled the congressional party in their direction. This has imperiled some of the remaining moderates either prompting their retirements or endangering their re-elections as they succumb to pressure to toe the party line even when it puts them at odds with many voters in their districts.

Party Identification

When Dwight Eisenhower ended twenty years of Democratic occupancy of the White House, among white voters in the South, Democrats outnumbered Republicans by more than eight to one (Black and Black 2002). The Democratic share declined from about 80 to roughly 50 percent in 1968 and remained there until Ronald Reagan ousted Jimmy Carter. When Reagan won re-election, Republican identifiers outnumbered Democrats, a pattern that persists today although neither party can claim the allegiance of a majority of the region's voters. Among white voters, however, Republicans outnumber Democrats in every Southern state (Knuckey 2015). In the Deep South, 57 percent of whites identify with the GOP compared with 26.8 percent who call themselves Democrats. Across the Rim South, Republicans outnumber Democrats among whites 49.1 to 36.9 percent. Based on the 2010 and 2012 CCES surveys, Democrats' strongest showings come in Arkansas and Florida where they trail Republicans by three and four percentage points, respectively.

The realignment had multiple causes. Some of the earliest Republicans, and these included individuals who set about recruiting with a disciples' zeal, came to the South in pursuit of business opportunities (Bullock and Kanso 2015). The leftward drift of the national Democratic Party that began with civil rights planks in the 1948 platform that fueled the breakaway Dixiecrat movement accelerated as President Johnson pushed the 1964 Civil Right Act and the 1965 Voting Rights Act through Congress. Upon signing the first of these, Johnson acknowledged to aide Bill Moyers "I think we just delivered the South to the Republican Party for a long time to come" (Oreskes 1989). Johnson's successor capitalized on the unpopularity of the civil rights efforts as he went about fashioning a Southern strategy that paid handsome dividends for the GOP beginning in 1972. Campaigning in 1968, Nixon promised to slow the push for school desegregation and to appoint conservative jurists—two promises designed to attract Southern conservatives (Phillips 1969). Progressive legislation prompted conservatives to break with their heritage and vote for Goldwater, Nixon, and Reagan.

Generational replacement played a role as Democrats whose loyalty to the party had been sealed during the New Deal saw their children give Reagan an iconic status comparable to what their elders had assigned FDR (McKee 2010). Trey Hood and his collaborators (2012) attribute the departure of conservative whites to the movement of newly enfranchised African Americans into the Democratic Party, which threatened conservatives' control of that entity. Whites could easily take over the hollow shell of the GOP and in doing so have a platform from which to continue articulating the same conservative values that had created a bifurcated Democratic Party at the national level. The political mobilization of religious conservatives provided foot soldiers for the emerging Republican Party. As liberals increasingly became the face of the Democratic Party nationally and took liberal stands on abortion and other social issues, Southern Evangelicals initially led by the Christian Coalition turned to the GOP (Rozell and Wilcox 1995; Rozell and Wilcox 1996).

The movement of religious conservatives into the GOP has paid handsome dividends as Evangelicals have become the most stalwart Republicans. The white Evangelical vote has become increasingly cohesive and in 2016, it gave Trump overwhelming support. As shown in Table 3.1 in the six Southern states in which exit polls were conducted, Trump got at least 80 percent of the Evangelical vote and in Georgia attracted a near unanimous 92 percent. In half the states the Evangelical cohesion equaled or exceeded that of African American who are the core Democratic constituency. In Florida and Texas the Clinton vote from African Americans equals the Evangelical vote for Trump. In the other states, the Evangelical vote for Trump exceeds the black vote for Clinton since Evangelicals outnumber African Americans. In the Carolinas the disparity is substantial. African Americans have been solidly Democratic at least since 1964. The Evangelical vote has become more united and constitutes a growing share of the electorate.

Table 3.1. African Americans and white Evangelicals: Core
constituencies for opposing parties

| | Black Support for Clinton | | Evangelical Support for Trump | |
	Vote for Clinton	% of the Electorate	Vote for Trump	% of the Electorate
FL	84	14	85	14
GA	89	30	92	34
NC	91	19	82	37
SC	94	19	88	44
TX	85	11	85	12
VA	88	21	80	25

Source: Compiled from media exit polls.

Republican candidates, especially those running for the presidency, often drew a share of the white vote that exceeded their percentage in terms of party identification. Eisenhower became the first Republican presidential candidate to get a majority of the white vote. Goldwater, who lost six Southern states, nonetheless outperformed Ike among white voters by winning 55 percent (Black and Black 2002). Nixon's Southern strategy attracted 80 percent of the white vote in 1972. Reagan, when campaigning for re-election, did almost as well Nixon in his bid for a second term, with 72 percent of the white vote.

White Southerners started voting for Republican presidential candidates long before they backed GOP nominees for other offices. Prior to 1992, large numbers of white Southerners regularly split their tickets (Bullock et al. 2005). But beginning with the Clinton election, white Southerners brought their vote for House candidates in line with their presidential party preferences.

As the GOP Crests, Democrats Begin to Rebound

Tremendous variability in partisan history exists among the states. In some, such as Alabama, Arkansas, Louisiana, and Mississippi, the

GOP has only recently consolidated its hold on the state legislature. Democrats also persisted longer in winning major statewide offices in these states. Arkansas and Louisiana were the last two Southern states to send a Republican to the Senate and the former had a Democratic governor as recently as 2014 while Louisiana chose a Democratic governor in 2015.

But in the Growth States including some in which the GOP scored its earliest gains, the tide has begun to turn. Democrats have rebounded furthest in Virginia, the first Southern state back in the 1970s, to have consecutive Republican governors.[10] In presidential elections, from 1952 to 2004, Virginia joined Arizona and Montana as the nation's most reliable Republican states. The Old Dominion, which had voted for the GOP presidential nominee in every election beginning with Eisenhower, except for Barry Goldwater in 1964, ended that tradition in 2008 when it cast 52.6 percent of its votes for Obama. Virginia stayed with Obama in 2012 and in 2016 Hillary Clinton beat Donald J. Trump by 5.4 points as she took 49.7 percent of the vote.

Democratic advances have not been limited to presidential contests. Four of the last five governors have been Democrats. Virginia elects only three constitutional officers statewide and as of 2018 each of these is a Democrat as are both of the state's senators. The state last elected a Republican senator in 2002. Republicans hold on to the state legislature by the narrowest of margins. Going into the 2017 elections for the lower chamber Republicans had a 66–34 advantage. Democrats did shockingly well, gaining 15 seats. They were on the verge of getting half the seats when a judge awarded a contested ballot to David Yancey, the GOP incumbent. That resulted in both Yancey and his challenger having an equal number of votes. Rather than stage a runoff, the names of the candidates were put into film containers that were swirled around in a bowl and Yancey's was drawn out giving Republicans a 51–49 advantage. The Republican hold on the Senate is equally small, 21–19. But for the districts drawn by Republican legislators following the 2010 census, Democrats might have already reclaimed the legislature. The narrow majority in the Senate marks a rebound for Republicans who lost their majority status between 2009 and 2015. Democrats secured a majority in the state's congressional delegation in 2018 when they flipped three seats in the course of defeating two incumbents.Democrats have also gained ground in Florida and North Carolina, both of which voted for Obama in 2008. That year North Carolina elected Democratic women to serve as senator and governor. Florida stayed with Obama in 2012 while North Carolina narrowly backed Mitt Romney. In 2016 both states lined up with Trump but the Tar Heel State ousted its Republican governor after he convened a special legislative session to block a Charlotte ordinance that would allow transgendered individuals to use restrooms in line with their current gender status. Trump's victory margin was 1.2 points in Florida and 3.7 points in North Carolina.

In Florida the Republican share of the House delegation slipped from a high of 19 in 2011 to 14 in 2019 even as the state gained two seats in 2012. In the state Senate Republicans held 23 seats in 2019 down from the peak of 28 and in the state House Republicans are down eleven from their highest point of 84. Contributing to the GOP losses was a constitutional amendment adopted in 2010 that limited the ability of the legislature to advance the interests of party and incumbents when redistricting. Overall the state remains Republican as demonstrated by the narrow GOP victories for governor and senator in 2018 but its toss-up status is in sharp contrast to a generation ago when Baron and Ujifusa (1991, 247) wrote, "of the megastates, Florida is now clearly the most Republican in national politics."

Demographic change has fueled the Democratic resurgence in these states. Here, as across the nation, Democrats thrive in urban areas. The magnet that is Washington, DC, has brought more well-educated young voters into northern Virginia. The Research Triangle has had a similar effect in North Carolina. (Hood and McKee 2010). In-migration to Florida is so pervasive that less than half its residents grew up there.Although not nearly as far along the way to a possible realignment, Georgia is increasingly targeted by Democratic hopefuls. While Georgia has not backed a Democratic presidential nominee since Bill Clinton in 1992, Trump won with 51 percent of the vote to Clinton's 45.9 percent. The margin in Georgia was among the twelve smallest in the nation. Georgia is poised to join Florida and North Carolina as a swing state. In Georgia, too, Democrats are counting on demographic changes. The Atlanta area attracts a diverse population of young adults with African Americans finding the city and its near suburbs especially appealing. The state's Hispanic population probably exceeds a million, and growing numbers of descendants of many Asian nationalities now live in metro Atlanta. The nomination of Stacey Abrams for governor in 2018 provided a test of an alternative theory about the more successful approach to locating the votes needed to fashion a statewide Democratic majority. Previous Democratic contenders such as 2014 gubernatorial candidate Jason Carter and senatorial nominee Michelle Nunn tried to win over white working class voters but managed to attract only 23 percent of the white vote.[11] Abrams's plan was to mobilize additional minority voters in order to overcome the 200,000 vote deficit that has denied Democrats victory in recent years. Despite Abrams's persistent efforts to increase black registration, figures as of June 1, 2018, show there to have been no change in the last decade with African Americans constituting 30.1 percent of the state's expanding numbers of registrants. But the increased African-American turnout for Abrams was impressive, and she narrowed the GOP advantage from 200,000 to 55,000 votes.

Democrats also hope that demographic change will make them competitive in Texas. The state is already one of the few in which whites do not constitute a majority and in time it may become predominantly Hispanic. If Hispanics become mobilized and if Texas Republicans do not return to George Bush's strategy of appealing to that community, Democrats in the Lone Star State could follow the path of their fellow partisans in California who, with the help of Hispanic voters, have dominated that state's politics for the last two decades.[12]

Weak performances in less visible contests may serve a function like the canary in the coal mine—signaling imminent change. In recent years, the GOP has lost ground in the state houses of five Growth States: Florida, Georgia, North Carolina, Texas, and Virginia. These are the states in which Democrats' prospects for recovery and perhaps even realignment are best. Comparing the number of Republican state house seats in these five states in 2019 with what the GOP had prior to the most recent election shows a loss of 54 with double-digit losses in Georgia, Texas and Virginia. A comparable analysis for the Stagnant States finds the GOP gaining eight.

Democrats also enjoyed advances in Growth State congressional delegations in 2018 as they picked up a total of eleven seats

Democrats made gains in each state except North Carolina where the Ninth District remains undecided after the 2018 results were thrown out due to questions about absentee ballots. In contrast there were no changes in partisanship in the Stagnant States' congressional delegations.

Republicans have just recently achieved dominance in four Stagnant States—Alabama, Arkansas, Louisiana, and Mississippi, all of which have lost multiple congressional seats since 1950. Republicans attained majorities in the legislative chambers of these states in 2009 or later. These states are not experiencing dynamic growth although Alabama and Tennessee have succeeded in attracting assembly plants for foreign automobile manufacturers. Large numbers of in-migrants from other parts of the United States or from other nations are not bringing new ideas into the political discussion in these states. The dominance of the GOP seems secure for the immediate future in these states.

An effort to graph the results for every state in the region would become a tangled mess. Therefore, Figure 3.8 shows the share of the

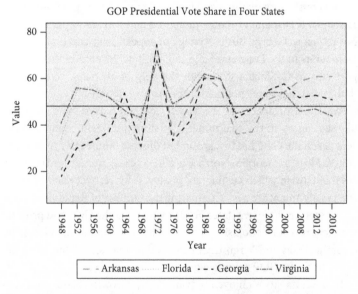

Figure 3.8. GOP presidential vote share in four states

presidential vote going to Republicans in four states. Of these, two (Florida and Virginia) show clear signs of a Democratic rebound. In Georgia support for GOP presidential nominees has declined since 2004. In contrast, in Arkansas, which is among the states most recently to become Republican, the GOP vote share has risen in each election since favorite son Bill Clinton ceased to lead the Democratic Party.

Figure 3.9 presents figures on the share of the seats in the lower chamber of the legislature for the same four states. For Virginia, the long slow climb to majority status that is almost uninterrupted until 2005 looks much like the pattern for state lower chambers Southwide presented in Figure 3.2. The Florida results largely parallel those for Virginia through 2003, but since then Republicans have done better in the Sunshine State although gains there have ceased. Georgia Republican success lagged that for Florida and Virginia but ultimately peaked at the same level as in those two

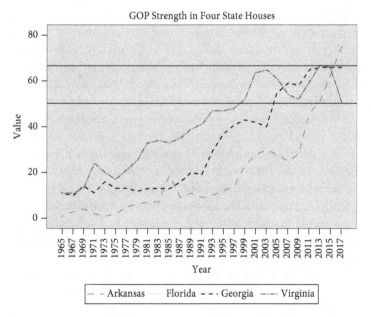

Figure 3.9. GOP strength in four state houses

states with roughly two-thirds of the seats. In contrast, the advance of Arkansas (for which data for Alabama, Louisiana, or Mississippi could be substituted with little difference) Republicans came at a slower pace than in the other states, with a delay of almost a generation in achieving majority status, compared with Florida and Virginia. However, like a new religious convert who displays exceptional commitment, the share of the seats currently held by Razorback Republicans now exceeds anything ever achieved in the other states as shown in Figure 3.9.

Already urban areas in the South, as in the rest of the nation, vote Democratic. Color-coded maps for recent elections show the South's urban centers as blue islands. The number of counties in urban areas that vote Democratic is growing. For example, the Atlanta metro area, the nation's largest at twenty-nine counties, had three Democratic counties prior to 2008. Obama's candidacy flipped three more counties. A seventh county voted Democratic for the first time in years in 2014. Although she did not campaign in Georgia or commit resources to the state, Hillary Clinton narrowly won the state's second and third most populous counties giving Democrats nine Atlanta counties. The exit poll showed Clinton beating Trump in metro Atlanta 76 to 22 percent and winning the Atlanta suburbs narrowly by four points. Democratic fortunes have also improved in northern Virginia. In 2000 only Arlington County and the independent city of Alexandria voted for Al Gore. In 2016, Clinton won these jurisdictions plus three more counties and a second independent city. Florida saw a similar expansion of Democratic strength albeit somewhat earlier than Georgia or Virginia. In the 1980s, only one county (Gadsden) supported the Democratic presidential nominee. When Obama carried the state in 2008 he did so with the support of fifteen counties at the center of six media markets including five counties in south Florida, the main counties in the Tampa-St. Pete area, two in the Daytona area, two in the Orlando area, and three in the Tallahassee area.

The only rural parts of the South not painted in scarlet are the remnants of the Black Belt that arced from east Texas to Southside Virginia. In some of these heavily agrarian counties black concentrations produce Democratic majorities.

Early Partisan Breakthroughs—Will History Repeat Itself?

If the history of the partisan realignment from Republican back to Democrat follows a pattern similar to that shown when Democrats supplanted the GOP, then the first statewide successes may come about more as a result of problems in the dominant party rather than as the product of a brilliant campaign by a candidate from the minority party. The factors that shape presidential elections usually differ from those that influence major statewide contests such as those for governor or senator. Unlike presidential contests where few voters have firsthand experience with the candidates, and the campaigns ignore most Southern states once their moment in the sun during the primary process passes, elections for statewide posts touch the lives of many voters. A share of the voters will actually have contact with candidates for major statewide offices.

The GOP achieved some of its victories during the decades of Democratic dominance as a result of one of five features, none of which was under the control of the challenger. These factors include hubris in the camp of the Democratic candidate, unresolved conflicts extending from the Democratic nomination process into the general election, scandal, incompetence, or a wave election. Looking to the future, it will not be surprising if one or more of these elements enables Democrats to win contests in states even when the electorate remains largely committed to the GOP. In the following paragraphs we provide examples of how these features advanced GOP fortunes in the past and, where appropriate, have opened the way for Democratic recovery.

All of the early dramatic GOP wins in Georgia came, at least in part, in contests that Democrats did not believe they could lose. Unknown IBM transplant from Indiana, Mack Mattingly, scored the first Republican statewide victory when he upset four-term Senator Herman Talmadge in 1980. Talmadge, who survived a vigorous primary challenge, took Mattingly so lightly that he did not return to the campaign trail until the Senate adjourned, did not replenish his campaign coffer, and despite having a massive information advantage, refused to debate his opponent despite the latter's skills being so underwhelming that he engaged a star high school debater as a coach. The second GOP Senate victory came a dozen years later when Paul Coverdale (R) knocked off Wyche Fowler (D) who had denied Mattingly a second term. Fowler, who had the reputation as an extraordinary campaigner, ran a "desultory campaign" in his re-election bid (Barone and Ujifusa 1993; Fenno 1996). Finally, when Sonny Perdue ended the Democrats' 130-year hold on the governorship, few in Governor Roy Barnes's camp thought that their man was in trouble.

An advantage enjoyed by the dominant party is a large supply of viable candidates. In contrast, the opposition is often delighted to have even one experienced candidate come forward. Open seats attract multiple quality candidates in the majority party, and in most Southern states that can extend the selection process into a runoff if no candidate secures a majority.[13] During the primary, candidates hoping to reach a runoff, temper their attacks on fellow partisans in case they need to seek support from candidates eliminated in the first round of voting. No such considerations restrain vicious attacks in the runoff and the rhetoric escalates. In some instances, the losing candidate, and even more often some of the loser's supporters, decline to support their party's nominee in November. Alabama's and South Carolina's first Republican governors succeeded when the loser of the Democratic runoff failed to become reconciled (Bullock and Kanso 2016).[14] A similar situation opened the way for Senator Jesse Helms (R-NC) following the defeat of the conservative Democratic incumbent by a more liberal member of Congress in the 1972 runoff. Yet another example involves the election of Floridian Claude Kirk who in 1967 became one of the first two modern Republican governors in the South. Kirk won after a bitter Democratic selection process saw the sitting governor rejected in a runoff. Although not the result of lingering animosity generated in a runoff, Virginia's first Republican governor benefited from disarray in the opposition. Linwood Holton enjoyed endorsement by the AFL-CIO and progressive organizations in Richmond, which in their opposition to the creaking Byrd machine, concluded that the Democratic nominee was no better and perhaps worse than the Republican (Bass and de Vries 1977).

Scandal contributed to Talmadge's 1980 defeat. Questions about misuse of public funds led the Senate to denounce the senior senator who then retreated to a facility to deal with alcoholism. In Tennessee, Lamar Alexander became the second GOP governor in modern times when it was revealed that the Democratic nominee, Jake Butcher, had ties to Bert Lance who had been forced out as President Carter's director of OMB over a banking scandal. Scandal also opened the door for Mike Huckabee to become governor of Arkansas. Huckabee, Arkansas's lieutenant governor, was planning a Senate bid when Governor Jim Guy Tucker (D) resigned after conviction for arranging $3 million in loans in connection with the Whitewater scandal that plagued the Clinton presidency.

One might contend that any time that the nominee of the majority party loses, incompetence somewhere—perhaps in the campaign or the candidate's efforts—played a role. A clear example helps account for the selection of Bob Martinez as Florida's second Republican governor. Barone and Ujifusa (1987) note that the Martinez victory came despite the "severe handicaps" he confronted. The blundering activities of the leading Democratic candidate opened the way for a more liberal nominee to emerge when Attorney General Jim Smith lost to a state legislator. Barone and Ujifusa describe the stops and starts of the Smith effort. As the more experienced and more conservative candidate, Smith might have been the Democrat's best choice. But he sowed seeds of doubt about his commitment and interest. He launched a campaign, then considered running as a Republican, next he joined the ticket of a Democratic gubernatorial candidate as the lieutenant governor,[15] then considered seeking a House seat before returning to his initial goal—running for governor as a Democrat. Democrats rejected Smith 51 to 49 percent in a runoff in favor of Steve Pajcic who lost to Martinez by ten points.

The 1980 wave election propelled three Republicans to the Senate from the South. Alabama (Jeremiah Denton) got its first GOP senator, while in Florida (Paula Hawkins) and in North Carolina (John East) a second Republican came to Washington to represent their states. These senators benefited from the enthusiasm that accompanied the Reagan candidacy, which also saw the addition of ten state legislators and one member of Congress to the GOP ranks in Florida and fifteen legislators and two members of Congress in North Carolina.

Some of the factors contributing to early GOP success have already featured in recent Democratic advances. George Allen (R-VA), who was frequently included on lists of likely GOP presidential candidates, lost his Senate re-election in 2006 after being filmed using a disparaging term to point out the individual hired by his opponent's campaign to track Allen's campaign. Louisiana elected a Democratic governor in 2017 in part due to David Vitter's (R) involvement with a call girl scandal in Washington.

Incompetence explains the defeat of North Carolina governor Pat McCrory in 2016. The governor called a special session of the legislature to reverse the decision of Charlotte's city council to allow transgendered individuals to use the restrooms in line with their gender identity. McCrory seriously misjudged public opinion. He could have waited until the regularly scheduled legislative session in 2017 to pass the legislation and in doing so eliminated an issue that easily accounted for the 11,000 votes by which McCrory lost.

Thus far no examples exist of a Democrat recently winning office because of a feud that persists among Republican runoff opponents. Nor can we point to a Democratic win attributable to GOP overconfidence. No Democratic wave has recently rocked the foundations of the Republican Party in the South. Nonetheless, we would not be surprised if examples of these kinds of problems that made Democrats vulnerable in the past come to the fore to trip up what appear to be likely Republican victories in the future.

Conclusion

Over the last half century or so, the South has experienced greater partisan change than any other region. As shown in Figure 3.2, Republicans went from holding few if any significant offices in the South to dominating the region's ranks of elected officers at every level. Change came gradually and at different paces for individual states. Republicans scored their first gains, often keyed to Dwight Eisenhower's presidential bids, in the Rim South. The candidacy of Barry Goldwater had a similar effect in the Deep South. Beginning in the mid-1990s, Republicans began winning majorities of legislative chambers, a task they completed at the onset of the second decade of the new century.

For decades the South had exceptional influence in Congress. Southerners, very few of whom drew Republican challengers, accrued seniority that prior to 1975 allowed a disproportionate share of them to become committee chairs. Especially after World War II, Southern Democrats often joined forces with Republicans to thwart the adoption of liberal initiatives. Conservative coalition

The South's disproportionate influence in Congress was balanced against the inability of any politician from the region to become president for more than a century. But once Southern politicians moderated their stands on race, they became eligible to hold the nation's highest office, and five have done so. With the demise of the solid Democratic South, the region has determined the outcome of five presidential elections since 1960. Several Southern states have become battlegrounds in presidential contests and at least two more are likely to enter the ranks of swing states in the future.

Virginia has come almost full circle. The state dominated by the Byrd Machine for decades when only conservative Democrats need apply for important positions (Key 1949), was where the late Alec Lamis observed that "party realignment struck with a vengeance" (1988, p. 145). Today the Old Dominion has become blue in statewide voting and seems likely to have a Democratically controlled legislature after the next election. The GOP grip on Florida and North Carolina has weakened to the extent that Democrats are competitive and win some major contests. At a minimum, GOP strength has peaked in these states and also in Georgia and Texas. In the next decade or so Democrats will win increasing numbers of statewide offices in these states, places where they have largely been shut out in recent years. Democratic gains in state legislatures and congressional delegations will be delayed where Republicans are in position to draw district lines following the 2020 census. Change back to the Democratic Party, like the earlier gains by the GOP, will come at different paces in different states.

In addition to its current role in presidential elections the realignment in the South was instrumental in ushering in the last quarter century of Republican dominance in Congress. The region's Growth

States may play a similar role if Democrats supplant GOP strength in Congress. Expanding their share of seats from the South may be essential for Democrats to improve on their performance where they have had a majority in the House in only three of the last thirteen congresses. As more Southern Growth States become swing states in presidential elections, the region will carry great weight in determining who leads the nation even if the occupant of the White House does not come from the South. A competitive South would provide an alternative path to Democratic victory less dependent on the Rust Belt.

4

The Changing Politics of Race in the South and Its Impact on National Politics

African Americans held center stage in the politics of the South long before most could vote. V. O. Key (1949) contended in his classic study of the region that its politics revolved around African Americans and that the white Southerners most determined to discriminate against blacks dominated political activities in the eleven states that had formed the Confederacy. Despite asserting that "Whatever phase of the southern political process one seeks to understand, sooner or later the trail of inquiry leads to the Negro," none of the thirty-one chapters in Key's 675-page treatise examines black political activity (p. 5). Five chapters, however, detail impediments, created by white Southerners, which succeeded in keeping their black neighbors from voting.

As Key was putting the finishing touches on *Southern Politics in State and Nation,* fewer than 10 percent of the region's African Americans could vote. Blacks sat in no Southern legislative chamber, and if they held any elective positions at all they served in the handful of tiny, rural, all-black towns. But, even as Key assembled the interviews and data that became his classic, the first hints of change began much like distant thunder on a summer afternoon—apparent to the attentive but unnoticed by most. Black registration in Georgia exploded from a few thousand to one hundred fifty thousand with one hundred thousand participating in the 1946 Democratic gubernatorial primary (Bullock et al. 2015). The spike in black political activity came as a result of the elimination of the poll tax and the white primary combined with an aggressive registration campaign that recruited black veterans in an unsuccessful effort to thwart the gubernatorial ambitions of racist

Gene Talmadge. To put Georgia's black registration in perspective, estimates of black registration across the South in 1947 stood at two hundred fifty thousand (Rodgers and Bullock 1972).

Black Political Advances

The 1946 Georgia experience proved atypical. In the two decades after World War II, black registration in the South grew slowly. By the late 1950s approximately a quarter of the South's black adults had negotiated the obstacles of literacy, understanding, and good character tests, paid a poll tax where applicable, and braved intimidation in order to sign up to vote. On the eve of the Voting Rights Act (VRA) in 1965, 43 percent of the region's black adult population had registered (Rodgers and Bullock 1972).

By universal consensus, the VRA is the most effective civil rights legislation ever adopted since it quickly wiped away the remaining barriers to black registration and voting. Thanks to this legislation the literacy test joined the white primary, grandfather clause, and poll tax on the rubbish heap of discrimination. Initially the literacy test ban applied to only seven Southern states, ones in which most adults had failed to vote in 1964. Another provision that applied to these states required that all charges impacting elections secure approval by federal authorities—either the attorney general or the federal district of the District of Columbia—prior to implementation. Subsequent versions of the preclearance provision expanded coverage to at least part of every Southern state except Arkansas and Tennessee as well as to all or parts of seven non-Southern states.

The 1965 VRA had an immediate and significant impact. Within a couple of years most black adults had registered in every Southern state. By 1970 two-thirds of the South's eligible black population appeared on registration rolls. The states that had been most repressive experienced the greatest change with the share of black adults registered increasing from 19 to 52 percent in Alabama and from 7 to 60 percent in Mississippi.

Many of the new black voters broke with the partisan inclinations of their parents. During the long decades when laws and intimidation kept most Southern blacks from the ballot box, to the extent that the region's African Americans had partisan preferences they remained loyal to the party of Lincoln. The Southern Democratic Party represented by Gene Talmadge (GA), Tom Heflin (AL), Cotton Ed Smith (SC), and Theodore Bilbo (MS), all of whom loudly preached white supremacy, held little appeal for African Americans. The father of Martin Luther King Jr., and the grandfather of Atlanta's first black mayor were both Republicans. But since the 1964 presidential election, when Lyndon B. Johnson, who had just secured enactment of a major civil rights bill, faced Senator Barry Goldwater (AZ), one of the few Republicans to oppose that legislation, Southern blacks, like their Northern cousins, have been overwhelmingly and unshakably loyal to the Democratic Party.

Half a century after King's death, Southern African Americans vote at about the same rate as whites and perhaps even higher in presidential elections (Bullock and Gaddie 2009). After each election the Census Bureau estimates registration and turnout rates by ethnic groups for each state. While these estimates have drawn criticisms, these are the only figures available for most states. In both 2008 and 2012, the Census Bureau estimates indicate that in at least seven Southern states the turnout among African American citizens equaled or exceeded the rate for white non-Hispanics. In some instances, the difference exceeded the margin of error. For example, in 2008, an estimated 72.6 percent of South Carolina's black citizens compared with 63.5 percent of whites voted. In 2012 estimated turnout among whites was above 80 percent in Mississippi and North Carolina and more than ten points higher than for whites. The full participation of African Americans has been a major force in transforming the region's—and national—politics.

Consequences of Increased Black Participation

The initial reaction of many Southern Democratic officeholders to an expanding black electorate was to double down in opposition to civil rights. That reaction proved short-lived as black enfranchisement transformed the Democratic Party pushing its officeholders leftward reducing the ideological distance between Northern and Southern Democrats. As the Democratic Party became more liberal it created space on the right end of the political spectrum, space quickly filled by an emerging Republican Party. However, as a viable option to the Democratic Party emerged, first in the Rim South during the Dwight D. Eisenhower years and then in the Deep South with Barry Goldwater's presidential bid, the most conservative whites started voting for Republicans. Defections initially came in large numbers in presidential elections then gradually in open seat contests for governor, senator, and legislators. Moreover, as a new generation of officeholders supplanted their unreconstructed predecessors, the overall voting records but also positions taken on civil rights legislation by congressional Southern Democrats shifted leftward (Bullock 1981). These new Democrats recognized the necessity of courting newly enfranchised blacks to replace their most conservative constituents who had defected to the GOP (Black and Black 2002).

As white politicians appealed for black votes one of the first changes involved rhetoric. Andrew Young, who in 1972 became one of the first Southern blacks elected to Congress in the twentieth century, explained the transformation. "It used to be Southern politics was just 'nigger' politics, who could 'outnigger' the other—you registered 10 to 15 percent in the community and folk would start saying 'Nigra,' and then you get 35 to 40 percent registered and it's amazing how quick they learned how to say 'Nee-grow,' and now that we've got 50, 60, 70 percent of the black votes registered in the South, everybody's proud to be associated with their black brothers and sisters" (Bass and de Vries 1977, 47).[1] In the short run, Key was correct. Broadening the franchise resulted in a more progressive Southern politics.

Black votes also elected black officeholders. In 1965 when Congress approved the first version of the VRA fewer than one hundred blacks held office in the South. By 2001 when the Joint Center for Political and Economic Studies did its last survey of black officeholders, Mississippi alone had almost one thousand. The bulk of these officeholders serve at the local level, which is hardly surprising since most public officials serve cities or counties. But not all are local. As of 2019, twenty-three African Americans represented the South in Congress, all but one of whom sat in the House. Texas had six, Georgia five, and Florida four.

All Southern states except Arkansas and Tennessee have at least one African American member of Congress.[2]

When the Democratic Party was stronger, a handful of African Americans won statewide posts beginning with L. Douglas Wilder being elected Virginia's lieutenant governor in 1985; four years later he became the nation's first popularly elected black governor. Blacks have competed successfully for statewide seats on collegial courts in Alabama, Georgia, Florida, and Texas.[3] In addition African Americans won multiple terms as constitutional officers in North Carolina and Georgia. Senator Tim Scott (R) represents South Carolina.

The first African American to serve in a state legislature in modern times won election in 1962 with the onset of the Redistricting Revolution. By the end of the decade as states redrew their maps to create majority black, urban districts, 39 black legislators served in the South. Half a century after the election of the first African American state legislator, the ranks had swollen to more than 350. Georgia and Mississippi have the largest black legislative caucuses. In 2018 the Peach State had fourteen black senators and forty-six representatives; Mississippi, which has a smaller legislature than Georgia, had one fewer black senator and thirty-six black representatives.

Until 1995, Democrats had majorities in every Southern legislative chamber, which meant that almost all black legislators belonged to the majority party. Black legislators had substantial influence over policy decisions in Democratically controlled legislative bodies especially on committees that they chaired. African Americans who chaired a rules committee, which set the agenda for a chamber, or a committee dealing with the budget exercised great power. As partisan margins narrowed in a chamber, black Democrats could exert even greater leverage, especially when blocking initiatives that they opposed. North Carolina's Dan Blue became the first black Speaker in a Southern lower chamber and currently African Americans occupy Democratic leadership posts in several chambers.

Today Republicans have majorities in every Southern legislative chamber. As Democratic ranks have dwindled, African Americans have become larger components of Democratic caucuses and now are a majority in fourteen chamber caucuses; with Hispanics they constitute a majority of the Democrats in three others. Despite enhanced influence in Democratic caucuses neither black nor white Democrats have much say in setting the agenda or designing legislation in majority-Republican chambers. Only when the GOP majority suffers defections and needs Democratic votes can African American legislators exert leverage.

In the electorate, weak white support for Democrats results in blacks now casting most of the votes in Democratic primaries. As white voters and white officeholders gradually shifted to the GOP in what Key defined as a secular realignment (Key 1959; Bullock, Hoffman, and Gaddie 2006), blacks exerted greater influence in Democratic primaries. Georgia blacks cast a quarter of the votes in the 1990 Democratic primary; a decade later that share had risen to 31 percent (Bullock 2014). In recent primaries, Georgia African Americans have accounted for as much as 62 percent of the Democratic vote with the white share down to a third. In 2014, nonwhites cast two-thirds of the votes in the South Carolina Democratic primary.[4] As the black vote share increases, it is hardly surprising that blacks have constituted a growing share of primary winners.

The black population has long since moved from the farm to town. Many of the South's largest cities have majority black populations. In 1973, Atlanta's Maynard Jackson became the first black mayor of a major Southern city. Birmingham and New Orleans soon followed and had black leadership for decades. Charlotte, Memphis, Dallas, Jackson, Houston, Richmond, and Savannah have also elected African American chief executives.

Once African Americans became an important component of the Democratic coalition in a community they began to reap benefits. The experience of Durham, North Carolina, where black voting came earlier than in much of the South was replicated in many communities as blacks bartered votes for public services and building projects (Keech 1968). At the local level, roads in black neighborhoods got paved, sidewalks got laid, water and sewer mains were extended, new parks were created and old ones spruced up. Black votes also translated into public jobs above the ranks of the janitorial staff (Button 1989). African Americans got hired by the police force and as firefighters and attained administrative posts in courthouses and city halls. Atlanta's Maynard Jackson demanded that minority contractors get a share of the work when the city built a new airport and on all other municipally-funded projects (Young et al. 2017). The presence of black officeholders on a collegial body often led to changes in the agenda with the African American members raising issues salient to their constituents that white officials had either ignored or not considered important (Greene 1991).

Not surprisingly once winning public office ceased to be a novelty, rivalries and divisions became visible among black leaders. In Alabama, Birmingham's first black mayor, Richard Arrington, created an organization, the New South Coalition, to challenge Rep. Joe Reed's Alabama Democratic Coalition. The two organizations often competed with opposing candidates in a wide array of contests across the state.

Redistricting

The decennial redrawing of legislative districts has been a mixed blessing for African Americans. The initial election of Southern African Americans to Congress and state legislatures came on the heels of redistricting (Handley and Grofman 1996). The Redistricting Revolution, which demanded that districts have equal populations, resulted in shifting seats from rural areas where barriers to black participation were highest to more tolerant urban centers. Large cities got so many state legislative seats that single-member districting assured that some of these would have black majorities and with the suffrage expanding pursuant to the VRA, African Americans could choose one of their own to represent them. New maps implemented in 1972 that created districts more than 40 percent African American saw Atlanta's Andrew Young and Houston's Barbara Jordan enter the House as the first blacks sent to Congress from the South since 1898.

Table 4.1 shows that the adoption of new plans often opened the door for additional African Americans to join state legislatures. The first black legislator elected to a Southern assembly since before World War I, Leroy Johnson, became a Georgia senator in 1962, the initial election held following a court order to equalize populations. Two-thirds of the growth in black representation came within two

Table 4.1. Redistricting and the addition of black members to Southern legislatures

	Initial	Redistricting Round				No. Blacks in 2017
		1970s	1980s	1990s	2000s	
Upper Chambers						
AL	0	2	2	0	0	6
AR	0	1	2**	0	0	3
FL	0	0	2	3	0	7
GA	1	0	2	1	0	14
LA	1	0	0	4	0	8
MS	0	2*	0	6	1	13
NC	0	0	0	2	0	11
SC	0	0	1	1	1	11
TN	2	0	1	0	0	3
TX	1	0	1	0	0	2
VA	1	0	1	1	0	5
Lower Chambers						
AL	0	11	2	8	0	27
AR	0	3	4**	1	0	12
FL	1	1	7	0	2	20
GA	7	5	0	4	3	46
LA	1	7	3	9	1	24
MS	1	11*	0	9	1	36
NC	1	1	8	4	0	24
SC	0	8	0	6	1	28
TN***	1	1	1	2	1	14
TX	2	6	0	1	0	16
VA	2	0	0	0	1	13

*Resolution of long running redistricting suit in MS brought the first two black senators and eleven more blacks to the House in the late 1970s.

**A lawsuit in the late 1980s prompted redistricting that added two blacks to the AR Senate and four in the House.

***Baker v. Carr brought the first black to the TN House, in the next election this pioneer was joined by five additional African Americans.

elections of the 1970, 1980, and 1990 censuses. The 1970 redistricting round introduced the first African Americans to three senates and three lower chambers. The ranks of black legislators grew by eleven in Alabama and Mississippi and by eight in South Carolina, seven in Louisiana, and a half dozen in Texas. Two senates got their first black members in districts drawn after the 1980 census. The Florida and North Carolina houses added seven and eight black members, respectively.

The redistricting of the early 1990s saw increases in black presence in most chambers. The catalyst for this increase was a new approach taken by the Department of Justice (DOJ) when evaluating proposals under Section 5 of the VRA as will be discussed in detail shortly. Plans drawn at the outset of the new century added few new black legislators as objectives of black caucus members changed. As of 2018, African American membership in most Southern legislative chambers was at all-time highs. In two senates and four houses, the share of seats held by blacks was at or greater than the black percentage in the state's adult citizen population.

To understand the dramatic increases in the early 1990s and the slowing a decade later requires a bit of history. Beginning with the 1970 round of redistricting, federal judges and the DOJ applied a non-retrogression test to plans from states subject to Section 5 pre-clearance.[5] To obtain necessary federal approval, a new plan could not leave African Americans worse off than the old plan. Federal authorities would reject plans that reduced the number of majority-minority districts or that cracked an existing district that, as a result of population shifts, now had a black majority. Non-retrogression meant that the number of majority-black districts would not decrease but would increase slowly if at all.

As early as the 1980 round of redistricting, African Americans joined with Republican legislators to oppose districting plans favored by the white Democrats who had majorities in all Southern legislative chambers. Blacks and Republicans wanted more seats and white Democrats filled the seats they coveted. The strange bedfellows' coalition became more common after the 1990 census as it challenged white Democrats who wanted districts with 20–40 percent black populations—too many Democrats to elect a Republican but not enough blacks to elect an African American (see, for example Holmes 1998). The African American–GOP coalition found an eager and powerful ally in the George H. W. Bush Justice Department. In the early 1990s DOJ augmented the obligation of Section 5 states to do no harm (non-retrogression) with an affirmative duty to draw additional majority-minority districts. Based on its interpretation of Section 2 of the VRA that called for minorities to have the same opportunities as whites to elect their preferred candidates, DOJ demanded the creation of additional majority-minority districts when feasible.

DOJ refused to approve congressional plans from Georgia and North Carolina that met the non-retrogression standard, citing as the reason that an additional majority-black district could be created. DOJ rejected these plans even though each state had added a majority-black congressional district. DOJ's refusal to pre-clear plans that did not maximize the number of majority-minority districts induced states to draw black districts before submitting their plans for approval. Since these new districts soaked up large numbers of African Americans, neighboring, bleached districts became much more likely to elect Republicans.

In their initial use in 1992, the new congressional districts performed as anticipated. African Americans gained three seats in Florida, two each in Georgia and North Carolina and one apiece in Alabama, Louisiana, South Carolina, Texas, and Virginia to increase their number across the South from five to seventeen. Republicans did even better and gained twenty-one seats that year. As reported in Table 4.2, the GOP made additional gains in 1994. In addition, after the GOP ended its forty years in the wilderness by taking control of the House under Newt Gingrich's (GA) leadership in 1994, five Southern Democrats defected to the GOP along with Senator Richard Shelby (AL). African Americans made no further gains in the 1990s and saw their ranks diminished in 1996 when Cleo Fields (LA) ran for governor rather than seek re-election to the House after his district was ruled unconstitutional and reconfigured since in drawing it the legislature, under DOJ pressure, gave greater weight to race than to other considerations.

By no means did all of the GOP gains come in districts from which large numbers of blacks had been removed but the bulk of the gains in

Table 4.2. Net changes in the numbers
of members in Congress in the
immediate aftermath of redistricting

Year	Black	Republican
1992	12	21
1994	0	8
2002	1	4
2004	1	6
2012	0	5
2014	1	3

the 1990s are directly attributable to the creation of the black-majority districts.[6] In addition to the seats in which removal of blacks tilted the partisan orientation, the unusually large disruptions caused by bizarre configurations needed to link distant black communities and form a district—districts given colorful names by the media such as the I-85 District (NC-12), the Zorro District (LA-4), the Bug Splat District (FL-3), and the Sherman District (GA-11) (because it went from Atlanta to the sea) separated nearby Democratic incumbents from many of their constituents. Several of these white Democrats did not have the time to establish rapport with their new constituents before the 1994 Republican wave election swept them to defeat (Petrocik and Desposato 1998).

African Americans made gains in the 1990s not just in congressional delegations but also in state legislatures as shown in Table 4.1. It is also likely that many of the objections DOJ registered to local redistricting plans in the early 1990s also stemmed from using Section 2 to demand creation of additional majority-black districts. The Supreme Court ended the push to maximize minority districts when it ruled that the DOJ lacked the authority to apply Section 2 considerations as part of a Section 5 evaluation. That ban came in a challenge from a Louisiana school district.[7] The courts invalidated plans creating majority-black congressional districts in Florida, Georgia, Louisiana, North Carolina, and Virginia for violation of the Equal Protection Clause since when drawing these districts race had taken precedence over all other considerations.[8]

The consequences of the redistricting efforts and litigation of the early 1990s extended beyond changes in the composition of legislative bodies. The protracted battles over how to draw districts increased pressure on the biracial Democratic legislative coalitions as blacks criticized their white fellow partisans for opposing the creation of more black districts while white Democrats accused their black colleagues of treason for working with Republicans.

In addition to helping lay the groundwork for GOP gains in the South's congressional delegations and state legislative chambers, the turmoil involved in drawing state legislative districts contributed to the environment that allowed Republicans to enjoy their first "permanent" takeovers of legislative chambers.[9] The 1994 wave election saw the GOP win majorities in the lower chambers of both of the Carolinas and take control of the Florida and Tennessee senates.

Following the 2000 census African American legislators rejected Republican overtures to resurrect the bipartisan coalition. With the potential for additional legislative chambers becoming majority GOP, black Democrats opted to help bolster their white fellow partisans rather than maximizing the number of majority-black districts. These efforts came too late to do much more than slow the ultimate takeover of Southern legislatures by the GOP.

African American ranks in Congress grew slightly in the new century. Under its 2001 plan Georgia became the first Southern state to send four African Americans to Congress. The much-maligned, mid-decade Texas redistricting enabled Al Green to defeat the incumbent in the Democratic primary and become the third African American in that state's delegation. New plans continued to pay greater dividends to Republicans, who picked up ten seats early in the new century, than to African Americans. The 2010 wave election swept in two African Americans who became the first black Republicans elected from the South since 1898. One of the Republicans, Tim Scott (SC), went to the Senate when Governor Nikki Haley appointed him to the vacancy created by Jim DeMint's resignation.

As of 2019, African Americans' share of the seats in four Growth States' (Florida, Georgia, Texas, and Virginia) congressional delegations closely matches their black population percentage. Two Stagnant States have no black representation in Congress, and in the other three states, each of which has a single black member of the House, that level of representation does not approach the black share of the state population. After the 2018 election sent an additional African American to Congress from Georgia and Texas, the region had twenty-two African Americans in the House and one in the Senate. All but Senator Tim Scott (R-SC) and Representative Will Hurd (R-TX) are Democrats.

African Americans in a Republican World

While Republicans had dominated Southern presidential elections for some time, not until the 1990s did they become the South's pre-eminent party for other offices. Since 1994, the GOP has controlled the region's congressional delegations, and more recently held most of the governorships and secured majorities in legislative chambers. Now that every Southern legislative chamber has a Republican majority, black influence has been significantly curtailed along with that of other Democrats. African Americans chair very few committees, and African Americans have little agenda-setting input.[10]

Partisan primaries are almost as racially segregated as the membership of Southern legislatures. Only a few states report information on participation in primaries by the race or ethnicity of the voters. Indeed, the vast majority of states do not gather racial or ethnic data on those who register to vote; therefore the analysis here draws on the few states that make the appropriate data available. African Americans cast most of the votes in Georgia's and South Carolina's Democratic primaries according to turnout data reported by these states. The dominance of black voters in Democratic primaries, the result of moderate and conservative whites voting in the GOP primaries, advantages liberals seeking Democratic nominations. Republican primaries remain almost exclusively the domain of whites. In South Carolina and Georgia, more than 90 percent of the ballots in GOP primaries come from whites.

A consequence of African Americans constituting larger shares of the Democratic primary vote has been the nominations of blacks for statewide offices. African Americans won nominations to challenge Republican senators in 2004 (Alabama), 2006 (Tennessee), 2008 (Alabama and Mississippi), 2010 (Florida, Georgia and South Carolina) and 2018 (Mississippi). In 2014 five African American women won nominations for statewide posts in Georgia. In 2018 African Americans won contested primaries to become the Democratic nominees for governor in Florida and Georgia. As of 2019, none of these black Democratic nominees for high profile offices had won a general election although two 2018 gubernatorial candidates came tantalizingly close with Florida's Andrew Gillum at 49.2 percent and Georgia's Stacey Abrams at 48.8 percent. When Democrats were still the dominant party African Americans won major executive offices in Virginia (governor and lieutenant governor), Georgia (attorney general and labor commissioner), and North Carolina (auditor). Now with Democrats in the minority in each Southern state except Virginia, black statewide victories have ceased with the exception of GOP senator Tim Scott (R-SC) and Virginia lieutenant governor Justin Fairfax.

Support for Barack Obama's 2008 presidential bid offers further insight into the impact of African Americans in Democratic primaries. Outside his home state of Illinois and the District of Columbia, Obama's largest primary victories came in Georgia, Virginia, and Mississippi.

The lily-white GOP primaries have often been dominated by religious conservatives. Estimates peg the Evangelical or born-again component of the GOP primary electorate at more than 70 percent in three Southern states while it exceeds 60 percent in four other states and falls below 50 percent only in Florida and Virginia (Skelley 2015).

Having African Americans as the core Democratic constituency and Evangelicals as the most loyal Republicans, promotes polarization.

As with primary participation, very few blacks support Republicans in general elections. White support for Republicans is not as cohesive as black support for Democrats, but is overwhelming and usually thwarts Democratic ambitions. In 2008, in Mississippi, Barack Obama as well as the Democratic nominees for U.S. Senate attracted less than 20 percent of the white vote (Bullock 2010). That same year in Alabama, Obama and the Democratic Senate candidate won about 12 percent of the white vote. Campaign consultants working for Georgia's 2014 Democratic Senate nominee, the daughter of former senator Sam Nunn, projected that if she secured 30 percent of the white vote and if blacks cast 30 percent of all votes, she would win. African Americans came close to meeting the target, providing 28.7 percent of the ballots. Michelle Nunn lost because she fell far short of the white vote she needed. The exit poll showed her with 23 percent of the white vote; even white women shunned her candidacy giving her only 27 percent of their votes.

Table 4.3 compares the strength of the core constituencies of the two parties in the 2014 and 2016 Senate contests where exit polls were conducted. In North Carolina, African Americans, 96 percent of whom supported Democrat senator Kay Hagan, cast 21 percent of the votes. The enthusiastic black support was more than offset by white Evangelicals who accounted for 40 percent of the electorate with 78 percent favoring Tom Tillis, who defeated Hagan. Across the states, blacks cast between 12 and 30 percent of the ballots and the Democrat always won at least 87 percent of those ballots in 2014 and more than three-fourths in 2016. However, in every case the Evangelical vote, which constituted from 20 to 52 percent of the total, provided the Republican candidate with a larger number of votes than the Democrat got from African Americans. In 2014 Texas Evangelical cohesion (86 percent) equaled that of African Americans (87 percent) nor was there a significant difference for South Carolina in 2016. Evangelical support for Republican Johnny Isakson in 2016 (89 percent) exceeded what blacks gave his Democratic challenger (79 percent).

With white Evangelicals so opposed to Democrats it is not surprising that even when the entire white electorate is considered, support for Democrats is modest. The three 2014 Democratic incumbent senators, Mark Pryor (AR), Mary Landrieu (LA) and Mark Warner (VA), did

Table 4.3. Black Democratic support versus white, Evangelical support in 2014 Southern Senate contests*

| State | % Black Support | | % White Evangelical | |
	%Black	for Democrat	%White Evangelical	Support for Republican
2014				
Arkansas	12	97	52	73
Georgia	29	95	39	86
Mississippi	30	92	51	82
N. Carolina	21	96	40	78
S. Carolina	26	89	40	81
Texas	12	87	32	86
Virginia	19	90	27	76
2016				
Florida	14	80	20	84
Georgia	30	79	34	89
N. Carolina	20	90	38	81
S. Carolina	19	90	44	88

*The 2014 exit poll for the Louisiana Senate election did not ask about Evangelical or born-again identification among white respondents so that state is excluded.

Source: Exit polls

best with between 31 and 37 percent of the white support. Non-incumbent Democrats performed worse with white support ranging from as little as 16 percent (Mississippi) to the one open seat where Michelle Nunn (GA) attracted 23 percent. While recent black state-wide nominees have lost, so have almost all of the white Democrats in recent elections across the South except for Virginia, the state in which the Democratic Party revival has progressed the furthest.[11]

Black candidates have won a few contests in districts that lack a black majority. White Democratic voters are about as likely to support a black Democrat as a white Democrat (Bullock and Gaddie 2009).

Several estimates have put the black share of the adult population needed for a black candidate to have an even chance of winning at less than 50 percent—far below the 65 percent of the population thought essential for a black victory circa 1980.

The success black candidates have had in attracting white votes has led to recent litigation brought by civil rights groups seeking to reduce black concentrations—just the opposite of 20–30 years ago when efforts sought to boost black concentrations. In the early 2000s, the Georgia Legislative Black Caucus attained near unanimity when agreeing to reduce the black percentage in their members' districts in an effort to maximize the prospects of white Democratic candidates in adjoining districts (Bullock and Gaddie 2009, 97). Bolstering white Democrats' fortunes was critical in the battle to prevent GOP takeover of the legislature. Civil rights veteran Rep. John Lewis (D-GA) explained why he supported the plan that reduced black concentrations. "[Georgia] is not the same state it was. It's not the same state that it was in 1965 or in 1975, or even in 1980 or 1990. We have changed. We've come a great distance. . . . It's not just in Georgia but in the American South, I think people are preparing to lay down the burden of race" (Lewis 2002). The Supreme Court approved the reduction but in renewing the VRA in 2006, Congress overruled the court.

Recent Concerns

Notwithstanding the gains registered by African Americans in the South, a new wave of litigation has swept the region. Civil rights groups have challenged the decisions of GOP legislatures that require a photo ID for those who seek to vote in person (Georgia, North Carolina, South Carolina, Texas, and Virginia), shortened the period for early voting (Florida and North Carolina), and maintained concentrations of African Americans in legislative districts (Alabama, North Carolina, and Virginia).[12] Other allegations point to a variety of activities that claim that public officials are acting to discourage minority participation. Some but not all of these changes have come in the wake of the *Shelby County v. Holder* decision, which eliminated federal supervision over changes in election laws in Section 5 jurisdictions.

Democrats have claimed that laws passed by Republican legislatures requiring that one present a government-issued photo ID to vote disproportionately burdens African Americans. Anthony Downs's (1957) calculus of the voting argument hypothesizes that any impediments will deter participation and those with the fewest resources will be most impacted. Plaintiffs contend that minorities, the elderly, and the youngest voters are less likely to have a driver's license, the most widely used state-issued photo ID, and therefore the requirement is discriminatory. Where an acceptable document is available for free and a variety of documents can be used, courts have approved these requirements. Data on turnout from Georgia and North Carolina, two states that collect information on race and ethnicity when voters register, provide little evidence that minority participation is seriously impeded, and this accords with scholarly research (Hood and Bullock 2012; Ansolabehere 2009).

The Census does surveys after every federal general election to determine how many Americans report having registered and gone to the polls. These data, while available for every state, suffer from problems such as inaccurate recall that plague any survey. A few states gather information on the ethnicity of their registrants and after elections issue reports showing the racial, gender, and age makeup of those who actually went to the polls. One of these states, Georgia, was among the first to require a photo ID in order to vote so that it has before and after data on the participation rates by ethnicity.

Table 4.4 reports that in 2004, prior to the photo ID requirement, 72.2 percent of African Americans registered to vote in Georgia cast ballots. Four years later when a photo ID was needed, 75.8 percent voted, followed by 72.6 percent in 2012 but down to 68.6 percent in 2016. In mid-term elections, black turnout increased from the pre-photo ID election of 2006 when it was 42.8 percent to 50.1 percent in 2010, 48.5 percent in 2014 and 53.8 percent in 2018. Perhaps even more telling since a multitude of factors can influence turnout, African Americans have cast a larger share of all ballots in every election since implementation of the photo ID law than before. In presidential elections, the post-election audit done by Georgia's secretary of state calculates that black ballots increased from about a quarter

Table 4.4. African American participation in Georgia elections before and after the photo ID requirement

		Georgia		
Before Photo ID				
	Presidential%	**Blacks as % of Turnout**	**Mid-Term%**	**Blacks as % of Turnout**
2004	72.2	25.4		
2006			42.8	24.1
After Photo ID				
2008	75.8	30.1		
2010			50.1	28.2
2012	72.6	29.9		
2014			48.5	28.7
2016	68.6	27.6		
2018			53.8	28.9
		South Carolina		
Before Photo ID				
	Presidential%	**Blacks as % of Turnout**	**Mid-Term%**	**Blacks as % of Turnout**
2008	76.2	30.6		
2010			48.6	28.5
2012	67.6	31.4		
After Photo ID				
2014			40.7	29.5
2016	62.0	28.2		

Source: Calculated from data posted on the website of Georgia's secretary of state and South Carolina Election Commission.

of the votes cast in 2004 to 30 percent in the next two presidential elections before dropping back to 27.6 percent in 2016. The decline is largely attributable to Hillary Clinton's frequently noted inability to connect with black voters. In mid-term contests the black vote share rose from 24.1 percent in 2006 to more than 28 percent in 2010, 2014, and 2018.

The lower portion of Table 4.4 provides results for South Carolina before and after implementation of a photo ID requirement. The Palmetto State has less experience with a photo ID, which was first implemented in 2014. South Carolina dichotomizes its registrants into white and nonwhite categories rather than having separate categories for blacks, Asians, and so forth as Georgia does. The results for mid-term elections do not show that requiring a photo ID reduced the relative rate of nonwhite turnout. While nonwhite turnout declined from 48.6 percent of this group's registrants in 2010 to 40.7 percent in 2014, white turnout fell even more so that nonwhites' share of all votes cast increased from 28.5 to 29.5 percent in 2014. The share of the 2016 vote cast by nonwhites (62 percent) is 5.6 points lower than in 2012 when a photo ID was not required. It is possible that the ID requirement accounts for some of this decline but it is even more likely that much, if not all of it, is due to the national decline in African American participation. The Census Bureau estimates peg black turnout across the United States in 2016 at 55.9 percent of the registrants, down from 62 percent in 2012 so that the 5.6 point drop in South Carolina is less than the 6.1 percentage point decrease nationally. The South Carolina decrease in the share of all votes from nonwhites from 2012 to 2016 (3.2 points) is a bit more than the Georgia decrease of 2.3 points.

Where available, early voting has proven popular with growing numbers of voters willing to stand in long lines to cast a ballot before Election Day. African Americans have found early voting especially appealing. Hillary Clinton's campaign encouraged and took heart from the throngs casting ballots in the days leading up to the 2016 election. Some black congregations have pews to polls or souls to polls operations where church buses take worshipers from the Sunday service to a polling place. Therefore, changes in early voting dates that eliminate Sunday voting are especially suspect in the eyes of civil rights groups. However, scholars who study the impact of early voting have concluded that while it allows voters to cast ballots at their convenience, it has not increased turnout rates (Stein 1998; Neeley and Richardson 2001; Gronke 2004).

Since very few African Americans vote for GOP candidates, Republican legislators have eagerly promoted districts with high concentrations of blacks, which usually elect African Americans. But with more whites now willing to support black Democratic candidates, African American candidates do not always need a black majority in the adult populations to win. Recent suits have challenged high concentrations of blacks in districts as packing, a well-known gerrymandering technique that results in "wasted" votes, that is, the preferred candidate wins but with far more votes than necessary. States defending these cases have explained that they maintained existing minority concentrations and even added to them because in 2011 they were still subject to Section 5 of the Voting Rights Act. The states feared that if they reduced the black concentrations DOJ would reject the plan for retrogression.

Virginia plaintiffs prevailed, which resulted in a new plan that sent a second African American to Congress in 2016 after blacks were shifted from the Third to the Fourth District. Challengers to the concentrations of blacks in Alabama state legislative districts also won. Reducing black percentages in districts has the potential to create additional Democratic-learning districts.

Another set of claims with strong partisan overtones see Democrats accusing Republicans of purging voters for nonparticipation or making it more difficult for voters to cast ballots. Recent controversies include a plan to close several precincts in a rural, majority-black Georgia county; demands that the names under which voters register exactly match the name on their drivers' licenses or social security card; and so forth. Much of this has played out in Georgia where Brian Kemp, the GOP nominee for governor who previously served as secretary of state (the state's chief election officer) was challenged by Stacey Abrams, the African American former House minority leader who been active in voter registration efforts for years. For years, Abrams charged Kemp's office with failing to process voter registration forms in a timely fashion.

Future

A widespread consensus anticipates that demographic changes underway will ultimately advantage the Democratic Party. As Barack Obama's 2012 re-election demonstrated, a Democrat who polls 80 percent of the minority vote can win the presidency with as little as 39 percent of the white vote nationwide. The demographic changes that bode well for Democrats in the presidential sweepstakes also point to a bright future for the party in several Southern states, all of which have sizable concentrations of minorities. Republican candidates have usually attracted small shares of the minority vote so as the electorate becomes more diverse, if Republicans do not fashion more encompassing appeals, the white electorate will ultimately become too small to sustain statewide victories. To the extent that younger and better-educated whites vote Democratic, it expedites partisan realignment. Recently Texas became one of four states that has no majority ethnic group. In time Florida, will join the Lone Star State as will Georgia as whites decline to a plurality. Texas is moving in the direction of having a Latino plurality. In 2016 Georgia joined Virginia, Florida, and North Carolina as toss-up states in presidential elections. Because of much lower turnout among Hispanics than whites or blacks, Texas will become competitive later than Georgia.

Once Democrats win not just presidential electors but also statewide posts, they will begin to position themselves to reclaim state legislative chambers. When Democrats achieve legislative majorities, African Americans, many of whom will have survived the years of GOP rule, will account for a disproportionately large share of the senior members and should advance to many of the leadership posts.

A Democratic resurgence, as discussed in Chapter 3, is more likely in the Growth States. The Growth States have already shown that they are more hospitable to the candidacies of minority candidates for higher offices. In every state, majority-minority districts regularly elect minorities, a pattern that is now decades old. The distinction among states is whether minorities can win statewide posts since those electorates continue to remain majority white.[13] Each of the Growth States has elected one or more minority candidates. Virginia chose Douglas Wilder first as lieutenant governor and four years later as its chief executive, and currently has an African American attorney general. Georgia has had African Americans serve as attorney general, and as labor commissioner, and they fill multiple seats on the state's two appellate courts. Florida has elected Hispanics as governor and senator and South Carolina has a black senator. Texas has an Hispanic senator and an African American has held a constitutional office in North Carolina. In the non-Growth states minority candidates have won Democratic nominations for statewide posts but none has yet won a general election.

In 2018 Democrats in two Growth States made serious bids to end years of Republican control of the governorship when African American candidates lost close elections. In Florida, Tallahassee mayor Andrew Gillum, who led in many polls until late in the contest, came up 34,000 votes short. In Georgia former House minority leader Stacey Abrams, who trailed narrowly throughout the fall, lost to Brian Kemp by 55,000 votes but came within 17,500 votes of extending the contest to a runoff since Georgia law requires that candidates win with a majority. The Georgia election was the closest gubernatorial contest since 1994. The margin in Florida was the narrowest in more than a century. Abrams and Gillum demonstrated that a black Democrat could compete effectively before a majority-white electorate. While Abrams came up short, the enthusiasm surrounding her campaign helped Democrats flip a congressional district and sixteen previously Republican state legislative seats. The congressional district Democrats picked up in Georgia, the Sixth, elected an African American even though it was less than one-seventh African American. Lucy McBath, who ran on an antigun platform as a result of her son having been the victim of a senseless shooting, benefitted from the mobilization efforts of the Abrams campaign. Florida Democrats picked up two congressional seats in the Miami area, one of which elected a Latina.

While African American candidates continue to encounter difficulties when competing statewide, the white electorate in the Growth States has shown a greater willingness to vote for blacks. Each Growth State has one or more African Americans elected to a high-profile post by a *majority-white* electorate. In statewide posts are South Carolina senator Tim Scott and Virginia's lieutenant governor Justin Fairfax. Congressional representatives from districts with black populations under 20 percent include Lucy McBath (GA), Will Hurd (TX), Marc Veasey (TX), and Colin Allred (TX). Congresswoman Val Demings (FL) won a district less than one-third African American. An African American has represented North Carolina's Twelfth Congressional District since 1993 but most of the time it has been majority white. The 2018 gubernatorial elections showed whites in Florida and Georgia more willing to support an African American competing statewide than in the Stagnant States. Results in these contests were so narrow that recounts were required. In contrast the Stagnant states of Alabama and Mississippi have had African American Democrats run for the Senate where they lost by more than 20 percentage points. In 2018 when Andrew Gillum (FL) and Stacey Abrams (GA) attracted 49 percent of the vote, Mike Espy, running for the Senate in Mississippi managed only 46 percent in a state in which the black population is more than twice as large a percentage is in Florida.

As the population in the Growth States becomes more diverse, the GOP reliance almost exclusively on white votes becomes more perilous. Republican campaign consultants recognize that for their party to retain majorities in Growth States but also in Congress, it will be necessary to devise a broader appeal that draws Hispanics and Asians into the party. Attracting significant African American support will prove harder given the close ties that the vast share of black political leaders and rank-and-file voters have developed with the Democratic Party over more than half a century. If GOP officeholders finally come to the realization that strategists such as Karl Rove have already reached, Republican legislators will stop pushing legislation widely perceived as hostile in ethnic communities such as denying driver's licenses to noncitizens and blocking access to state universities to those brought illegally to the United States as children. If Republican officials persist in penalizing those who did not arrive in the nation legally, this hostility will hasten the time when Democrats will start winning statewide offices and expanding their legislative ranks.

Race and ethnicity remain major organizing features in Southern politics but concern about race and denying rights to African Americans no longer is at the center. Half a century after King's assassination, Southern politicians spend far more time courting outside investment than in concocting new stratagems to keep African Americans from the ballot box, good jobs, or good schools. Federal legislation opened the way first to the ballot box and later to seats on collegial bodies ranging from city and county councils to the state and congressional delegations. African American voters have replaced whites as the basis for the Democratic Party in the region. The ability of blacks to get desired policies depends heavily on which party wields power. When Republicans dominate office holding as they do today, Democrats regardless of ethnicity have little success in promoting their agendas. Democrats attempt to use minorities as the basis for challenging the kinds of steps that parties use to enhance their position—actions very similar to what Democrats did in the decades in which they enjoyed majority status. But even so, the repression that denied basic rights to minorities in the South when Key wrote has long since been swept aside, gone with the wind.

5

The Rise of the Christian Right
in the South and Its Impact
on National Politics

v. o. Key (1949) famously noted that the "black belt" that stretched across the South defined its politics before the civil rights revolution. The "Bible belt" has defined much of the region's politics since then. Although most observers trace the rise of the modern Christian Right to the late 1970s, the Richard M. Nixon Southern strategy in 1968 included an important dose of outreach to conservative Evangelical and Catholic voters in the region.

The transformation of the South away from one-party dominance by the Democrats and toward strongly Republican is one of the pivotal political events in the United States since the tumultuous events of 1968. Entangled in this story is the role of religion, particularly the emergence of the Christian Right as a social and political force. The most important social movement of the late twentieth/early twenty-first century in the United States has its origins in the South, and it has become a major political force nationally.

What began in the South as a fragmented and disorganized movement, widely dismissed as extremist, eventually grew and developed into a politically mature and sophisticated interest group in national politics. It is impossible to discuss the transformation of Southern politics and its impact on the nation without an examination of the critical role played by the Christian Right.

The Origins and Development of a Social Movement

The Christian Right "is a social movement that attempts to mobilize evangelical Protestants and other orthodox Christians into conservative political action" (Wilcox and Larson 2008: 6). This mobilization is rooted in a traditional approach to particular social issues, especially abortion, school prayer, and gay rights. Once mobilized, Christian Right activists challenged existing party structures to address these issues. Democrats and Republicans have subsequently coalesced around these morally charged issues, with the Republicans gaining the support, and sometimes the scorn, of the Christian Right. The relationship between the maturing social movement and the Republican Party has at times been difficult. Yet, as the Christian Right has sought influence within the party, it has often built coalitions with other party interests and sometimes produced harmonious results.

Politically the Christian Right has waged a defensive campaign against a changing society. As American society has become more socially progressive, the Christian Right's escalating rhetoric has often been delivered with a Southern twang. There is something distinctively Southern about the Christian Right. The South is disproportionately Evangelical Christian when compared to the rest of the nation, and being Southern is a significant predictor of personal attachment to the Christian Right, even when religious and socioeconomic variables are controlled (Hood and Smith 2002). Also, the South has been the breeding ground for most of the leading Christian Right figures (for example, Rev. Jerry Falwell, Rev. Pat Robertson, Ralph Reed, Rev. Mike Huckabee, George W. Bush, Rev. Jerry Falwell Jr.), as well as the birthplace of two of the most critical institutions within the history of the Christian Right: the Moral Majority and the Christian Coalition.

The Christian Right has deep roots in the South due to the region's long history of overlap between religion and politics. As the South moved slowly beyond racial strife, that helped set the stage for Christian Right issues to rise to prominence and eventually transcend the region.

Southern Religion and Politics

The strife of civil rights in the 1960s had a devastating impact on political coalitions throughout the South. Republican gains in the region
began at the presidential level, but eventually the party took advantage
more widely. The Democrats were fractured, split between African
Americans and some white progressives, and traditional, conservative opponents of social change. As a result, a "creeping" realignment
(Bullock 1988) that combined critical and secular elements created
two-party competitiveness in the region.

Religion played a key role in changing partisan coalitions in the
South, with Evangelicals over time aligning with the GOP. That did
not quickly happen. GOP presidential nominee Richard M. Nixon
reached out to Southern Evangelicals in 1968, but his potential gains
were limited by the third-party candidacy of native son Southerner
George Wallace who won five Southern states in the presidential election. Born-again Southerner and Democrat Jimmy Carter attracted
substantial Southern Evangelical support in his successful presidential
race in 1976. Religious conservative disappointment with President
Jimmy Carter's social policies combined with strong outreach to
Southern Evangelicals by GOP presidential candidate Ronald Reagan
reconfigured the political landscape in 1980. Religious conservatives
centered in the South, but nationally as well, have had their political
home in the Republican Party ever since. The once "solid (Democratic)
South" by the 1990s had become the solid Republican South.

The Christian Right's activism is rooted to a large degree in the belief
that its values are under attack. Evangelical Christians hold relatively
few positions of major influence in the mainstream media, academia,
government bureaucracies, and the public education establishment,
which are precisely the institutions conducting the perceived assault
on "family values." The gap between Evangelical values and those of
the broader culture grew in the 1960s and 1970s era of the sexual revolution, student protests, and gay rights—all of which are antithetical
to the Christian Right's values.

The Christian Right's activism can be traced in large part to two key
Supreme Court decisions of those decades: *Engel v. Vitale* (1962) where
the Court ruled that school-sponsored prayer was unconstitutional

in public schools, and *Roe v. Wade* (1973) in which the Court struck down the abortion laws of many states. These rulings caused Christian Right activists to focus their energy on the Supreme Court and to make Court nominations, and hence presidential elections, an important part of the movement's agenda. Donald J. Trump's presidential victory in 2016 is owed in no small measure to the vacancy that was on the Supreme Court and the GOP nominee's promises to social conservatives to appoint "pro-life" justices.

The Christian Right's Southern roots began to push toward the surface in the 1970s, though the movement would not breach it until 1979, with the founding of the Moral Majority. Before then there were signs that the region's persistent overlap of religion and politics was moving away from race and civil rights and toward issues that would later define the Christian Right. Two events show the possibilities and pitfalls for the Christian Right that was about to emerge.[1]

During the 1974-1975 school year, Kanawha County, West Virginia, witnessed an ugly, sometimes violent textbook controversy. Alice Moore, the wife of a Fundamentalist minister, spearheaded a protest of sex education in the local schools and later defeated an incumbent for a seat on the school board. When the board later approved a new batch of textbooks that had been adopted by a committee of teachers, Moore expressed dismay and outrage, charging that the books undermined authority, promoted profanity, eroded confidence in America, and promoted a secular humanistic viewpoint. Though she could not convince the board to do anything, she continued to speak out at local churches and board meetings. Several groups were organized in support of her position, including the Concerned Citizens of Kanawha County, which was made up primarily of churches in the area. A counter group, the Citizens for Quality Education, organized and was led by a local Episcopalian rector, who was later labeled "Lucifer" by the protestors. When the new school year began, about one-fourth of the district's parents kept their children at home in protest, and picketers in the area obstructed school buses and local coal mines, where thirty-five hundred miners engaged in a sympathetic walkout. The school board made some concessions, but eventually voted to return nearly all of the books deemed offensive to the curriculum, with the remainder to be placed in school libraries. A lawyer for the Heritage Foundation came to speak on behalf of the protestors, as did Citizens for Decency Through Law spokesman Bob Dornan (later elected to Congress), Rev. Carl McIntire, and others. Local mayors in the area hatched a failed plan to secede from the county, and private schools began to spring up, enrolling two thousand students by the fall of 1975 (Faigley 1975; Page and Clelland 1978).

While educational controversies remained at the fore for the Christian Right, an additional conflict foreshadowed the quarrels that would later help define the movement, especially in the South. In January 1977 the Dade County (Florida) Commissioners voted 5–3 to approve an ordinance that prohibited discrimination against homosexuals in housing, public accommodations, and employment. The popular singer and Florida citrus spokeswoman Anita Bryant and the Archdiocese of Miami had unsuccessfully urged the measure's defeat. Bryant then formed Save Our Children, an organization devoted to repealing the measure. As Bryant successfully organized a petition drive to call for a referendum on the matter, the issue attracted enormous national attention. The ordinance was overwhelmingly repealed (69 to 31 percent) in the high-turnout referendum.

Although the eventual national prominence of the movement took many observers by surprise, in retrospect it is clear that a convergence of circumstances led to the breakout of the Christian Right. That convergence happened when the leaders of the New Right joined with Falwell and other leading Christian Right figures to embrace the presidential candidacy of Ronald Reagan, a unique conservative who had strong appeal among various factions of the Right, including anticommunism, antigovernment, and religious conservative groups.

The 1980 Reagan landslide, combined with the GOP takeover of the U.S. Senate, stunned many political observers. Most polling data leading up to Election Day did not predict this Republican windfall. Political observers looked for credible explanations of the unexpected size of the GOP victory. The Moral Majority leader, Rev. Jerry Falwell, said that he had the answer: his movement had succeeded in awakening what he called the "sleeping giant" of U.S. politics, Evangelical conservatives. Falwell claimed that several million previously apolitical Evangelicals had gone to the polls in 1980 and thus transformed the U.S. electoral landscape in favor of the Republicans. Falwell and his

Moral Majority became staples of media coverage of politics. The once dismissed Christian Right became known as potential kingmakers.

As much as the Christian Right movement previously had been dismissed too readily, it also received perhaps too much credit for the growing GOP fortunes during the 1980s Reagan-Bush era. Numerous factors contributed more to the GOP's rising fortunes than the rise of Evangelical activism surrounding social issues. The state of the economy and foreign policy had much larger influences on the elections than the issues that mobilized the Christian Right. Reflecting this reality, the Reagan and George H. W. Bush administrations relegated social issues constantly to the back burner, much to the frustration of religious conservatives.

Nonetheless since the period of Christian Right mobilization in the 1980s, the movement has achieved some important victories. To be sure, the movement has not achieved its ultimate goals at the national level, such as overturning *Roe v. Wade*, restoring spoken prayer in public schools, and stemming the advancement of gay rights. But at the state and local levels, especially in the Deep South states, the movement has been very influential both in elections and in affecting a number of policy areas, particularly abortion and public education.

The rise of the Christian Right has had a major influence on reconfiguring the Southern political landscape. The "Solid South" was once predominantly white Protestant and dominated by the Democratic Party. In the contemporary era, the white Protestant South is the most reliable core of the Republican Party. And as the South has become increasingly diverse and less distinctive, coalitions of minority groups, including religious minorities, anchor the Democratic Party in the region.

According to the Pew Research Center, white Protestants account for slightly less than half of the adult population in the South (http://www.pewforum.org/religious-landscape-study/region/south).   But it is the fast-growing "high commitment" Evangelicals who are the largest portion of that group, and they constitute about one-third of the Southern adult population generally (See also Green et al. 2010: 288). As the national Democratic Party became wedded to civil rights and abortion rights, high-commitment white Evangelicals increasingly moved to the Republican Party. William Martin (1997: 207) recounts that the final breaking point for many of these voters was discontent with the policies of the Carter presidency. Election data show that since the early 1980s, this group has remained firmly in the GOP camp, and even in presidential elections that favored the Democrats in the national popular vote, such as 1992, 1996, 2000, 2008, 2012, and 2016, the Republicans' Evangelical base in the South remained solid.

After Reagan's 1980 victory, Democrats nationally stepped up their efforts to attack the GOP for its increasingly deep alliance with the Christian Right. Such efforts fueled increased talk of "culture wars" in the United States, and thus deepened the attachment of Southern evangelicals to the Republican Party.

In 1984 the Democratic presidential nominee Walter Mondale repeatedly tried to characterize Reagan as a social issues extremist by linking him to the Virginia pastors Falwell and Rev. Pat Robertson. Mondale frequently quoted a Falwell statement that suggested that the Christian Right would get to effectively pick the next two Supreme Court judges if Reagan won re-election. Reagan not only swept the South and the white Evangelical vote by huge margins, but he nearly swept the country.

In 1988 Robertson ran for the GOP presidential nomination, and although he raised a record amount of money for the campaign and won some state caucuses, he never seriously threatened to win. Robertson's campaign showcased the difficulties of Christian Right mobilization on behalf of a movement leader, even in the South. Although the movement brings many new voters and intensified energy to the GOP, it is not sizable enough itself to carry a candidate such as Robertson, who lacks appeal to other party constituencies. Robertson badly lost key races in the South, such as South Carolina and his home state of Virginia, to Vice President George H. W. Bush, a moderate. In the fall campaign Democrats tried to tar Bush, the eventual GOP nominee, as being too cozy with the Christian Right. Bush had actually surprised many observers when he switched from pro-choice to pro-life and when he adopted a number of other social conservative positions that conflicted with his earlier stated views on issues. Yet again the GOP won an Electoral College landslide, sweeping the South and maintaining the voting strength of the Evangelical core of the party.

The Christian Right took center stage during much of the 1992 election season. The political commentator Pat Buchanan, a hero of cultural conservatives, challenged incumbent George H. W. Bush's renomination. Although the president easily won the GOP contest, Buchanan carried enough votes and support on the Right to earn a major speaking role at the national party nominating convention that summer in Houston. On one evening, Buchanan and Robertson had prime-time speaking roles, and the resulting derisive commentary by critics about "family values night" was widely circulated by the media and likely hurt Bush's re-election prospects.

The 1990s saw an increased effort by Democrats to reach out to values voters and to try to compete more effectively in the South. The 1992 presidential nomination of Arkansas's governor Bill Clinton along with the choice of U.S. senator Al Gore (TN) at least strengthened the Democrats' Southern credentials. By winning four Southern states that year, the Democrats made an important dent in the GOP's regional base. In 1992 and 1996 the Democratic ticket carried the Southern home states of Clinton and Gore. Louisiana was the only other Deep South state to vote Democratic in both of those presidential elections. The party won Georgia in 1992 and Florida in 1996 (Bullock 2018: 3).

Clinton and Gore did not concede the "family values" voters to the Republicans. Indeed, the Democratic ticket reached out to the more conservative white Evangelical South on a number of issues in order to lessen the GOP natural advantage with that constituency. The Democrats championed some culturally conservative positions, such as installing the V-chip on televisions to allow parents to regulate the content of what their children can watch, advocating mandatory school uniforms in public schools, and originating the White House office that gave rise to faith-based federal programs. The Democratic ticket succeeded in both election cycles at holding down the size of its losses in the South and somewhat with holding down its losses among the large white Evangelical electorate in crucial parts of that region.

Southern and faith-based politics combined in the 2000 Democratic ticket of Vice President Al Gore and Senator Joseph Lieberman (CT). Gore possessed the potential advantage of his Southern roots, whereas Lieberman, an observant Jew, convincingly spoke the language of faith-based politics. Yet the new decade brought back the solid Republican South and overwhelming white Evangelical backing for the GOP in presidential elections. In the 2000 contest, the GOP nominee, Governor George W. Bush of Texas, carried all of the Southern states, including Gore's home state Tennessee by a comfortable margin (51 to 47 percent).

It was the Republican nominating contest in 2000 that highlighted the power of the GOP's evangelical core in the South. Bush made overt appeals to religious conservative voters in his campaign, and his closest challenger, U.S. senator John McCain (AZ), ran as a secular conservative who had some appeal to party moderates and independent voters. In this hard-fought contest, McCain largely won the non-Southern states with small Evangelical populations, whereas Bush swept the South and the Evangelical vote by impressive margins. In all of the contested states before Bush secured the nomination, the exit polling data showed that McCain consistently defeated Bush among non-religious-right-identifying voters. But in all of these contests, Bush won a commanding majority among voters identifying with the religious right (Rozell 2002). The religious right component of the GOP, along with Bush's overwhelming appeal among those voters, carried the Texas governor to the presidential nomination. It was in the key states in the South, especially the critical contests in South Carolina and Virginia, where Bush made his move toward certain nomination.

Nonetheless it was unexpected and very surprising to many observers that the Evangelical share of the total vote turnout in the 2000 general election had declined from the previous election cycle. To be sure, Bush overwhelmingly won the Evangelical vote, but the mobilization of that group was unimpressive. Going into the 2004 reelection campaign the president's chief political strategist, Karl Rove, had commented that the key to Bush's victory would be to mobilize the several million Evangelical voters who had dropped from electoral participation in 2000. The Bush re-election campaign thus made a strong push to identify and motivate conservative Evangelicals in several key states in the Electoral College.

The 2004 election became known as the year of the "values voter." According to a widely reported exit poll, when given choices among many factors affecting their decisions on Election Day, the number one choice among voters was "moral values." And among those who chose this option, an overwhelming majority voted for President Bush (Rozell and Das Gupta 2006). The president won close to four-fifths of the evangelical vote and he swept the South. Even though the Democratic ticket of Senators John Kerry (MA) and John Edwards (NC) featured a Southerner, the party made no inroads in the region.

With the white Evangelical vote so solidly Republican, there has been increasingly less talk over time about the Democratic Party regaining its previous hold on the South, although Virginia has moved strongly Democratic-leaning and several other Southern states have become highly competitive. For years conventional political wisdom said that Democrats could not win the presidency without winning the South. Until Barack Obama's historic election in 2008, the only Democratic candidates to win the presidency since John F. Kennedy were southern Baptists (Lyndon B. Johnson, Jimmy Carter, and Bill Clinton). Among those successful candidates, only the pure South ticket of Clinton and Gore won the White House without winning the South in the Electoral College. The conventional wisdom thus shifted to Democrats merely needing to hold down their losses in the South— as happened in 1992 and 1996—in order to win the White House.

Obama's 2008 and 2012 presidential victories seemed to recon-figure the political landscape. In 2008, the Democratic nominee took the White House while winning only three Southern states: Florida, North Carolina, and Virginia. Despite a distinct lack of enthusiasm for the GOP nominee, Senator John McCain (AZ), the white Evangelical vote in the South was remarkably strong for the McCain-Palin ticket. If anything attracted these voters to the ticket, it was the vice presi-dential selection of Governor Sarah Palin of Alaska, an unapologetic social conservative.

Religion and the South played prominent roles throughout the 2008 campaign season. With no incumbent president or heir ap-parent seeking the nomination, the GOP race featured a large field of candidates. One surprisingly strong candidate was a Baptist minister and former Arkansas governor, Mike Huckabee. His appeal among Evangelical voters proved to be a major impediment to the candidacy of former Massachusetts governor Mitt Romney, a Mormon. Both candidates possessed social conservative credentials, certainly much stronger than those of McCain. The competition between those two men opened the door for McCain to prevail and showcased an important divide on the Republican right wing.

Polling data revealed the challenge for Romney seeking the party's nomination. A significant minority of voters admitted that they were less likely to vote for a candidate for public office who is a Mormon. This finding was especially strong among Evangelical voters.

As the campaign shifted to Super Tuesday, with twenty-one GOP primaries and caucuses, the contest featured McCain, Romney, and Huckabee as the major contenders. Romney got swept out of the race, losing the evangelical vote and all of the Southern states to Huckabee. But McCain emerged as the victor, winning nine states. Romney won his home state (Massachusetts) as well as Alaska, Colorado, Montana, North Dakota, and Utah. But Huckabee prevailed in Alabama, Arkansas, Georgia, Tennessee, and West Virginia. McCain, though long reviled within the Christian Right, performed nearly as well as Romney with Evangelical voters (Smidt et al. 2009: 93). Because of Romney's strong social conservative credentials, his ultimate defeat at the hands of Southern Evangelicals led many to wonder whether his Mormon faith remained the key factor in his disappointing showing in the nomination race.

A good measure of the continued GOP hold on white Evangelical Southerners was McCain's strong showing in the region. In his previous presidential run, in 2000, he had made some overheated comments against social conservative leaders Robertson and Falwell. Although the senator later spent considerable effort to repair the political damage to his reputation among the Evangelical core of the GOP, for many of those voters he remained suspect. Yet in the election, despite considerable Democratic outreach to Evangelicals, McCain held this core group nearly as solidly as Bush had in 2004. Additionally, despite Evangelical reservations about Romney as the GOP nominee for president in 2012, he fared well with white Evangelical voters who may actually have been voting more against Obama than enthusiastically for Romney.

The presidential victories for the Democrats in the 1990s and in 2008 and 2012, as well as the many disappointments with some Republican administrations' policies, showcase the limitations of the religious conservative movement's placing heavy emphasis on helping the GOP win the biggest prize in U.S. politics. The Christian Right has been thwarted time and again on national policy over the past three decades of movement activism, leading many to wonder if the emphasis on the presidency and national politics had been misplaced. Indeed, there is much evidence to suggest that the Christian Right has had some significant policy victories at the state and local levels in parts of the country where there is a hospitable environment for social conservative views.

The 2016 election changed the national fortunes of the Christian Right through the unlikely candidacy and presidential victory of Donald J. Trump. Whereas social conservatives expressed deep disappointment with past GOP administrations' generally tepid commitment to the social issues agenda, Trump has put the agenda of the Christian Right at the center of his presidency. Leaders and activists of the movement are delighted with Trump's appointments and policies, and some have said that he is by far the best president the movement has ever had. Many nonreligious conservative Americans have expressed puzzlement at the intensive support that the Christian Right has given to a man of such poor personal character, but ultimately what matters to his supporters much more is that they believe he keeps his commitments on policy.

Religious conservatives voted overwhelmingly for Trump and were key to his victory in the general election. Trump won white Evangelicals—the core of the religious right—with 81 percent of the vote. He actually outperformed GOP nominees Mitt Romney and George W. Bush. Impressive as well, he won the Catholic vote, which, unlike several of the latest previous presidential elections, broke more strongly in favor of the GOP nominee than the overall popular vote (Gayte, Chelini-Pont, and Rozell 2018).

As this is written in the twenty-fifth month of Trump's presidency, there is much to suggest that he has fulfilled many of his commitments to religious conservatives who supported him so strongly. And give credit to those who placed their bets with candidate Trump: on the singular most important decision of lasting import of his young presidency, he delivered two solid conservative jurists, Neil Gorsuch and Brett Kavanaugh, to the U.S. Supreme Court. That is a big victory for the religious right and its supporters have every reason to consider their backing of candidate Trump to have been a very good decision for that reason alone. And given the advanced ages of several other Court members and the actuary tables, it is likely that President Trump will be able to further swing the Court to the right and the possibility of *Roe v. Wade* being overturned is more real than ever now.

There are other important successes so far for religious conservatives. In his first days in office President Trump by executive action reinstated the so-called Mexico City Policy, derisively known as the "gag rule"—the ban on federal dollars for international family planning agencies that provide abortion-related counseling or services. That issue has long been a political football, put in place by President Ronald Reagan and either overturned by every Democratic president or reinstated by every Republican one since. Commitment to this ban has since the 1980s been a core issue for religious conservatives.

Although most secular Americans associate the religious right almost exclusively with the abortion issue, social conservatives are intensely mobilized for action on issues of schooling. They have a strong antipathy toward what they perceive as an anti-religion and even anti-Christian ideology pervading public education. President Trump has scored with social conservatives in his appointment of Betsy DeVos as secretary of education, and in his strong support for so-called "school choice." The president has committed to supporting policies that promote education vouchers—a highly controversial idea but one that resonates with religious conservatives who believe that funds used for public education should be available for parents instead to send their children to private religious-based schools. Such a policy would begin to partially defund public schools while transferring tax revenues to religious academies—a long-standing goal of the religious right.

Numerous other actions of this presidency resonate with the religious right. There are appointments of social conservatives such as Ms. DeVos and Department of Housing and Urban Development (HUD) Secretary Ben Carson. The president controversially issued an executive order travel ban on citizens from seven Muslim-majority nations. Although the legal fate of the ban at this writing remains uncertain given court challenges, it featured a special dispensation for persecuted Christians. Vice President Mike Pence—his very selection itself an affirmation of Trump's pro-life credibility—prominently participated in the annual March for Life procession. No other presidential administration has had that high-level direct participation in the March.

In short, religious conservatives feel validated in backing Trump for president and believe that he will continue to pay back their loyalty. And with some historically poor public approval ratings, the religious right is the singular, unwavering loyal constituency of President Trump.

Virginia: Case Study of Southern Transition and the Christian Right

The South in particular has been fertile ground for Christian Right activism. A focused analysis of the movement's impact in an important Southern state showcases the influence of social conservative activism in that region.

By some accounts Virginia is the birthplace of the modern Christian Right. It was the home of Falwell and the Moral Majority as well as Pat Robertson and the Christian Coalition. Prior to the rise of the Moral Majority, Falwell had gotten a taste of political activism in Virginia. For example, in 1978 he was a leading figure in a successful pastor-led campaign to oppose a referendum to legalize pari-mutuel betting. Falwell and other religious leaders raised substantial revenue to fund an expensive print and television advertising campaign against the referendum. Emboldened by their success, conservative religious leaders promised to stay politically active in the state (Rozell and Wilcox 1996: 42). Falwell called the effort a portent of "future endeavors together" (Gatins and Briggs 1978).

Robertson is the son of a former U.S. senator from Virginia, and thus he did not share Falwell's earlier reluctance to become engaged in political activity. In the 1970s Robertson was the major impetus behind promoting the political career of a religious conservative candidate who successfully won a seat on the Norfolk City Council and then placed third in the 1978 Democratic Party nomination race for U.S. Senate (Rozell and Wilcoix 1996: 37–39). Robertson's and

Falwell's activities in the 1970s attracted a lot of attention in Virginia, and thus their rise to national political prominence was perhaps not all that surprising to residents of the Old Dominion.

Christian Right activism in the 1980s in the state showcased the movement's limitations. Having achieved a taste of success, there was a substantial upswing in movement activity in the Republican Party in the 1980s. Yet in the statewide election years of that decade (1981, 1985, 1989), a GOP era at the presidential level, the Republicans lost every race for governor, lieutenant governor, and attorney general. In each case a candidate with close ties to the Christian Right headed the GOP ticket, and the Democrats successfully exploited these connections in order to characterize the Republicans as extremists. Statewide polls during this decade showed Falwell and Robertson to be hugely unpopular figures, and Democratic strategists understood that linking these leading pastors to GOP candidates made Virginians less likely to vote Republican.

The problem for the GOP was that the Christian Right leaders and activists had pushed party candidates to be openly committed to the movement's most controversial issue positions. The implied, and often direct, threat was that social conservative voters would sit out the election if a candidate adopted moderate positions on social issues. Having adopted positions on abortion and school prayer that many voters considered extreme, the GOP nominees had trouble appealing to voters outside the conservative party base. It is no exaggeration to say that social issues positions and close ties to the Christian Right were major factors in the defeats of the GOP candidates in the state in the 1980s elections.

The experiences in Virginia in the 1980s seemed to suggest that if the Christian Right was a liability to the GOP in a culturally conservative Southern state and the home of the Moral Majority and Christian Coalition, then the movement probably could not be successful anywhere. But the 1990s saw a major reversal of the fortunes of the Christian Right in the state. A new generation of Christian Right organizations was becoming active. These organizations and their leaders avoided many of the problems that plagued the earlier incarnation of the Christian Right. Learning important lessons from the defeats of the 1980s, they modified their tactics, marketed their message more effectively, organized at the grass roots, and fostered interdenominational cooperation and political coalition building (Rozell and Wilcox 1996: 58–90).

The turning point was the 1993 election. Republican gubernatorial nominee George Allen ran as a mainstream conservative and won a massive landslide, whereas the lieutenant governor nominee, a former Moral Majority leader and fundamentalist pastor, Michael Farris, badly lost. Unlike in the 1980s elections, Christian Right leaders did not push Allen to take extreme positions on controversial issues as a condition for supporting him. Rather the leaders had become much more politically savvy and not only gave Allen the leeway to sound like a social moderate, but heavily worked the activist core of the movement to trust Allen's true commitment to their issues.

The success of this strategy showcased the potential for the movement to become an increasingly powerful force in state politics in the South. With a state law that limits governors to nonconsecutive terms, Allen was succeeded by the 1997 GOP nominee James Gilmore. Although the party lost the gubernatorial elections in 2001 and 2005, the GOP made major gains in the state legislature, and a number of social conservative initiatives, such as parental notification for minors seeking an abortion, became law.

Throughout the period of the 1990s and 2000s, the Christian Right had become thoroughly mainstreamed into state politics, and it seemed no longer a political liability for a candidate to be closely aligned with the movement. Indeed, in 2009 the GOP nominated a genuine Christian Right candidate for governor, Attorney General Robert McDonnell, a graduate of Robertson's own Regent University. McDonnell focused on economic, not social, issues and he won the governorship in a landslide election, thus demonstrating the long-term success of the Christian Right strategy to moderate its rhetoric and tactics to the point where the movement no longer seemed threatening to Virginia voters. While Democrats tried to pin the label of social issues extremist on McDonnell, he emphasized jobs, the economy, and sound fiscal management of the state.

Christian Right success in statewide elections though reversed in 2013. The GOP nominated for governor a highly outspoken and controversial social conservative Ken Cuccinelli, who lost a razor-tight margin election to former Democratic National Committee chair Terry McAuliffe. That election was like a throwback to the 1980s era of GOP campaigns in the state, as the party nominee in 2013 did nothing to soften his social issues positions and rhetoric. Remarkably, with so much baggage, Cuccinelli still nearly won, which probably owed much more to lack of enthusiasm for McAuliffe than support for the GOP nominee's issue stands.

Then in 2017 the GOP lost a massive landslide having nominated a once noted party moderate, Ed Gillespie, who ultimately ran instead as a Trump Republican staking far-right positions on immigration and controversial social issues. It is difficult though to attach any meaning to the importance of the social issues in this campaign given that the election featured a massive "blue-wave" anti-Trump turnout that not only swept the Democrats to all three statewide offices, but fifteen GOP incumbents were turned out of their state legislative district seats. Turning to the 2018 midterm elections, in Virginia three Republican incumbents in the House of Representatives lost their seats, again attributable mostly to an anti-Trump Democratic wave turnout.

This brief account of the Christian Right's rise and eventual successes in Virginia is telling of the movement's evolution in the South and in some other regions as well. But it is primarily in the South where the Evangelical core of the GOP is strongest, and that region has played a key role in tipping the balance of U.S. politics for decades.

The experiences of the movement in Virginia provide a model for how the Christian Right can continue to play an active and influential role in the politics of the South in the future. Virginia nonetheless is becoming a difficult battleground for the strongly Republican-leaning Christian Right, as the state has trended increasingly Democratic in the past decade due in large part to demographic shifts that have favored the more liberal and fast-growing urban regions that now dominate Virginia elections. Indeed, no Republican has won statewide in Virginia since 2009.

As some of the Southern states begin to trend in a similar direction as Virginia, though not so rapidly, the politics of that state provide an important lesson for the Christian Right as it seeks to adjust its strategies to the emerging two-party competition in some parts of the still Republican-dominated South.

Conclusion

The future of the Republican Party appears heavily intertwined with the Christian Right and the South. The conservative Evangelical vote is the solid core of the GOP in the region. The success of the party nationally depends heavily on its ability to maintain its strong Southern base. As demographic trends point to an increasingly fast-growing minority population in the South, the GOP actually needs to both hold its Evangelical core and broaden its appeal among other voters. Over time the Evangelical vote cannot carry the GOP in the region. At the time of this writing, it appears that few in the GOP have figured out that reality.

To appeal successfully to different groups as well as conservative Evangelicals, the GOP needs to find candidates who can reach out to diverse populations. Former governor Robert McDonnell of Virginia is a possible model candidate for the future of the Christian Right and the GOP in the South. When he ran for governor in 2009 as the GOP nominee, Democrats made much of his close ties with the Christian Right and his social issues conservatism, that he had graduated from Pat Robertson's university, and that he had a past record of some extremist views on the role of women in the family and the workplace. Yet McDonnell did not run as a Christian Right candidate, and indeed he downplayed the social agenda and focused on jobs and the economy. He spoke the secular language of politics very effectively and skillfully deflected questions about his personal views on women and the social issues agenda. More important, he had accumulated a record of public service nearly two decades long, as a state legislator and attorney general of Virginia. During that long stretch, he established a credible record on a variety of policy issues—an important shield against Democratic accusations that he was a narrow social issues extremist. Voters looked beyond his past controversial positions and judged him on his overall record of service and as a skilled candidate in the campaign. As a result of his success, many observers began to suggest a national political future for McDonnell, but all such discussion ended when he became embroiled in accusations of financial misdeeds.

Another telling case is the surprisingly strong showing of Mike Huckabee in the 2008 GOP presidential nomination campaign. Although a social conservative, Huckabee struck a populist tone on economic issues, and he often sounded more like a traditional Democrat than a conservative Republican. Most candidates with Christian Right appeal have also aligned with other conservative interests, such as lower taxes, smaller government, pro-gun rights, and anti-labor union. But as the demographics of the South transition toward much higher percentages of Latino, African American, and other minority group voters, the GOP cannot rely so heavily on its white conservative Evangelical base to carry the region. As some minority groups exhibit more socially conservative views than whites on a variety of issues, from abortion to gay rights, and also have higher levels of religious participation and observance, religious conservative candidates such as Huckabee present an intriguing possibility for the future of the GOP in the South.

The election of Trump in 2016 though is the most telling. Like Huckabee in 2008, Trump ran as a social conservative but with a populist economic message on international trade and restoring declining industries in coal and the manufacturing sector. He attracted widespread working-class white support not only in the South, but also in the critical upper-Midwest states that delivered him the Electoral College victory. His ability to put together a coalition of support that included a strong social conservative turnout for him gave Trump his surprise Electoral College win despite losing the popular vote to Democratic nominee Hillary Clinton.

For the Democrats, reaching out to conservative Evangelicals in the South remains a tough sell. The party in recent years has done far more religious outreach than in the past. There have been direct efforts to reach evangelicals on such issue areas as the environment and the economy, anchored by data showing that young Evangelicals are much less conservative than their parents in these issue areas. There has also been much more "God talk" coming out of the party's candidates than in the past. Despite these efforts, the white Evangelical vote in the South remains heavily Republican and the Democrats have mostly benefited in recent election cycles from big turnouts among their traditional constituencies. At the state and local levels, though, many so-called "Blue Dog" Democrats have succeeded by positioning themselves to the right of the national party on a variety of issues, including the social policy agenda.

Regardless of the standing of the two major parties in the South, the Christian Right will remain an important player in the region's politics. Although in the past there has been much speculation about the future of the Christian Right as a formidable force in U.S. politics, the movement has shown remarkable endurance. Especially in the South, there is no reason to believe that the Christian Right will disappear any time soon from the political scene. It remains an anchor of the Republican Party in the region and gives the national party a strongly Evangelical and Southern accent. From the national perspective, the key question is whether the Republican Party can succeed with a white Southern Evangelical base of support. The Christian Right has successfully made the Republicans the social conservative party, and yet the country is moving in an increasingly progressive direction on the social issues agenda.

6

New York Sybarite Conquers the South

Trump, Race, and the Southernization of American Politics

The surprising victories of Donald Trump in the Republican primaries and the general election of 2016 would have been impossible without his remarkable support among Southern white voters. This chapter seeks to measure whether and how race affected Trump's triumphs, and to assess the role of the South in his victories. It concludes that white racial resentment helped Trump overcome numerous handicaps in his remarkable victories. This effect seems to work differently in the primary and the general election. In the primary, it allowed him to succeed in the South against native South rivals who often lacked many handicaps that Trump brought to the Southern contests. In the general election, racial resentment assisted Trump nationwide, as well as in the South.

One of the puzzles of the Trump victory is that he won every primary held in the South, with the exception of Texas, which had a favorite son candidate in Senator Ted Cruz. The South was Trump's strongest region in terms of number of statewide victories, although not in percent of the electorate. For reasons covered later on in the chapter, Trump's strength in the South was surprising.

The Trump campaign and the 2016 electoral context were highly unusual. Never since the dawn of modern polling had the two major political parties nominated candidates with negatives as high as Clinton and Trump; even though Trump's were higher, it was unknown how the electorate would respond to two such unattractive nominees. Obviously, 2016 also featured the first major party nominee who was female, which also could have unpredictable consequences for voting. The election also took place in the aftermath of eight years of America's first black president. The broader national context also included a forty-year increase in partisan polarization, a process that continued to erode political norms and expectations during the 2016 campaign.

While every presidential contest features some unique features, 2016 was unlike any campaign in American history across a host of measures. This should cause researchers to be cautious about applying expectations and models based on earlier elections. Still, it is inevitably where our study must begin.

Moreover, some of the unusual aspects may guide our research. The number of campaign discourse norms that Trump violated defy quantification. His withering assaults on opponents, media figures, Gold Star families, Hollywood stars, and others were unprecedented, as was his use of social media to deliver many of them. His regular assaults on "political correctness" allowed him to say and do things that prior politicians could not have, even had they wished to. And this includes racial rhetoric likely to create media firestorms that would have immolated other campaigns. So many controversies erupted constantly around Trump that the public's attention could never firmly focus on one or two "deal breakers." And the media's constant attention to each new controversy contributed to Trump's dominance in the media. Moreover, many Trump voters seemed to consider his style and brusque verbiage as brave truth telling.

Many of Trump's crudest expressions had racial connotations, such as when he labeled some Mexican immigrants as rapists. Did his rhetoric on race, and his presentation of self as a bold, angry (white) voice bravely airing politically incorrect truths, ignite white racial prejudice and resentment? Did his rhetoric combine with his past history of racist statements around "birtherism" and his policy stances on racially sensitive questions to further inflame race? Did that racial resentment manifest along one of the oldest fault lines in American politics, that between the South and the rest of the nation, the only divide in American politics that led to full-scale war?

Primary Elections, the South, and Trump

The post-reform dominant paradigm of American presidential primary elections suggested that Trump would fail in his effort to take the 2016 GOP nomination. If the "party decides" or in other words, unelected party elites effectively truncate the choices of primary voters down to candidates acceptable to the establishment, then Trump could not win. However, this interpretation of the party decides model (Cohen et al. 2008) has been challenged as simplistic (Silver 2016; Friedersdorf 2016). The authors neither claimed that party elites were all powerful nor always unified. Martin Cohen, one of the founders of the party decides school argued that in fact the GOP in 2016 wasn't unified at all, as measured by endorsements, perhaps the key variable in the model (Economist 2016). Another interpretation that was particularly deft, put forward by political scientist Dan Drezner among others, was that the influence of the paradigm resulted in the paradigm not predicting correctly. Every other GOP candidate assumed Trump could not be the nominee, and so none of them did the things that would have been necessary to stop him. No one wanted to be the agent of the inevitable decline in Trump, for fear that being seen as responsible for his loss would put that person at a competitive disadvantage with the remaining Republicans (Economist 2016). After all, the eventual nominee when Richard Gephardt and Howard Dean went after each other in the 2004 Democratic primaries was John Kerry. Trump's reputation as a counterpuncher, who had the ability to destroy anyone who attacked him, seemed to insulate him from some of the usual attacks. Everyone wanted to inherit his fanatically loyal following, rather than be the one who took him out.

Issues also matter in primary elections, perhaps even more than in general elections because of the obvious absence of partisan cues. Thus, Trump's victory may also have related to a number of issue positions he took, or to his overall style/approach to politics, or both. His issue positions were quite different from establishment Republicans: opposition to the Iraq War, opposition to entitlements cuts, occasional advocacy of universal healthcare, strongly anti-free-trade views, and an open support for positions seen by many as racist or racially tinged, such as angry attacks on Black Lives Matter, denigrating Mexican immigrants as rapists and criminals, attacking a Mexican American judge as incapable of being fair because of his ethnicity, and so on. His style was perhaps even more of a break with primary norms, as he refused to have a normal set of foreign and domestic policy advisors. Consequently, the positions he had tended to be little more than slogans, and he neglected many campaign norms in favor of Twittering to his followers.

Trump may also illustrate the media's dominance in primary elections, an argument famously made by political scientist Tom Patterson (1994). In the absence of partisan cues, which dominate in the general election, voters would need guidance from the media. Patterson argued that the media judged candidates based on electability and competence, and their judgments had effectively replaced or at least challenged the party establishment's prior role as gatekeeper of nominations. But here again, Trump represents at least a partial challenge to an existing theory. If the media are the gatekeepers, their overwhelmingly negative coverage of Trump failed to disqualify him with the Republican electorate. In 2016, while Trump received as much as $2 billion worth of free media (LaFrance 2016), it could hardly be described as positive overall.

Thus, whether party elites or media elites play dominant roles, the victory of Trump serves as a serious challenge to either idea. He won despite opposition from much of the GOP establishment, and despite negative stories in the media that would have doomed prior candidates.

Another aspect of Trump's candidacy that surprised many election experts was his strength in the South during the primaries. Trump's handicaps in the South began with his thick New York accent and his lack of regional affinity overall. Inarguably the most culturally distinctive region of the country, and the one that positions itself most in opposition to East Coast bastions such as Manhattan, the South had a history of coolness toward Northeastern candidates in both the Republican and Democratic primaries. Northeastern Republicans such as Rockefeller, Ford, Romney (in 2008 and to a lesser extent 2012), and Giuliani, or Northeastern Democrats such as Dukakis, Tsongas, Bradley, and Dean all found Southern primaries to be unfriendly environments compared to the rest of the country (Mayer

2002). Another way of saying this is that the South has had, perhaps more than any other region, a preference for candidates who share their accent, dominant conservative Christian faith, or worldview.

The South has been the most conservative region in both parties' primaries, where candidates who pay the most homage to conservative (in GOP) or moderate (in Democratic) positions tend to do well, ceteris paribus. Trump had previously been for gun control, and radically pro-choice. Moreover, he had not too long prior been a Democrat, and had made donations to leading Democrats, including his most likely opponent, Hillary Clinton. The South is sometimes considered the "buckle on the Bible Belt" and had been notably unfriendly to more secular Republicans such as John McCain (in 2000). Yet Trump was famously nonreligious, with no record of regular church attendance in his fifty years of adult life. Nor did his public comments on religion during the primary show familiarity with the most basic aspect of Christian doctrine, such as the necessity of confession and forgiveness, or even the name of a New Testament book (it's not "two" Corinthians for anyone whose been awake in a Southern church for a few Sundays). Trump had also committed one of the most deliberately public acts of adultery in modern American history, as he engineered coverage in tabloids of his putative sexual prowess while cheating on his first wife. "Best Sex I Ever Had" screamed a large headline at a time when his children by his wronged spouse were old enough to read (Mayer 2016). Trump had also cheated on his second wife, and then married a woman who had modeled nude (Kranish and Fisher 267–268). He appeared (clothed) in a soft-core porn video, and owned casinos. Post-election, one Christian Right leader was heard to say that Trump was granted a "mulligan" for his alleged infidelity pre-presidency. But given the number of sexual misconduct problems Trump has, including more than twenty allegations of sexual assault or harassment as well as affairs that came to light after the election, one with an adult film star immediately following the birth of his fifth child with his third wife, this isn't a one stroke golf "mulligan"; it's letting him win the Masters Tournament. In the region of the country where born-again Christians are the largest part of the Republican electorate, such a record was predicted by many to render Trump almost unelectable in the nomination fight.

Another aspect of Southern culture that Trump did not fit is the expectation that candidates will at least pay homage to its cultural values. George Herbert Walker Bush, a transplanted Northeastern who rose up in Texas politics, was still having to do that during his presidential races. A powerful scion of wealth and New England elitism forced to attest to his love of pork rinds and country music (Mayer 2004): what better demonstration of the South's ability to demand cultural obeisance? Other candidates in both parties have gone hunting in Southern environments to try to appeal to the region's gun-philia. Southern political culture is also distinctive in its reverence for the military; it features a higher participation rate in the military than any other region, and has more military bases per capita. Prior non-Southern candidates have tried to use their military records to buttress their appeal in the South, but Trump avoided the Vietnam draft (four student deferments and then one for "bone spurs" that neither hindered his athletic prowess in high school or college prior to the draft nor affected his post-draft life in the slightest.) Trump was caught on tape stating that avoiding venereal disease while promiscuously dating in New York in the 1970s was "my Vietnam," a comment that might have been problematic for any other candidate running in the South. Trump, perhaps to his credit, did not engage in Bush-style pandering to alleged Southern sensibilities. Why he got away with that is worthy of examination.

The reason may be another Southern political tradition: racism. As V. O. Key (1949) argued seventy years ago, so dominant was race in the thinking of the Southern white voter that the political character of Southern states and counties can be effectively predicted by their level of black population. Key claimed that when black population rose high enough, almost all other political considerations took a back seat to the need among white Southerners to maintain racial unity and white power. The importance of racial issues in Southern politics is an old story in American politics (Carter 2000; Black and Black 1989; Mayer 2002). As the most racially outspoken white candidate to credibly seek a major party nomination since George Wallace challenged Lyndon Johnson in the 1964 Democratic primaries, Trump in the GOP primaries can be seen as a test of the puissance of race as an issue, in the South and throughout the nation, given all his other handicaps.

Race and American Elections

Race has played a vital role in every presidential election since at least 1960 (Mayer 2002). This is true in years, such as 1964 or 1968, when it may have been the single most important domestic issue, and in years such as 1960, 1976 or 2000, when it was deeply submerged on the national agenda. Race shapes the national and state party system as well as state political environments. Whites, blacks, and Hispanics have reliably different voting preferences, particularly in the context of presidential primaries and the general election. Since 1964, a majority or plurality of whites have voted Republican in the presidential election, and the vast majority of blacks have supported Democrats. Since 1972, the black vote has been central to the Democratic primary contest; the black vote has supported a losing candidate in the Democratic nomination fight only once (1988). This was true again in 2016; without the black vote, Hillary Clinton would not have defeated the unexpectedly strong challenge from Bernie Sanders.

Other ethnic/racial groups also mostly remain part of the Democratic coalition. Hispanics tend to vote Democratic, although the division among them by national origin is vital to any understanding of Hispanic politics. The Republican primary electorate has remained incorrigibly white during this same period, with Hispanics and Asians playing an occasional role in only a few states.

This is not to suggest that racial issues, racial attitudes, and racial realities have not undergone change during this period. Change has been vast and almost continuous. The enfranchisement of blacks in the American South radically altered the nature of the politics of the region and indeed the nation. And within the broader American public, racial equality became at least the stated goal and belief of most white Americans (Schuman, Steeh, and Bobo 1985). Yet this racial equality as goal/belief does not translate among most white voters to support for policies that might address grave inequalities in economic, social, and political life (Bobo 1998; Dixon, Durrheim, and Tredoux 2007). Southern whites, particularly Southern white men, remain far more subject to racist attitudes about the inferiority of blacks (Kuklinski, Cobb, and Gilens 1997).

How racial issues can be activated in a campaign has also been studied. Some argue that racial issues can be primed by subtle or not-so-subtle deployments of racial symbols. Political scientist Tali Mendleberg argued that the use of the ads such as the famous Willie Horton one in 1988 could give racial cues to white voters that would prime their ambient prejudices against blacks (Mendleberg 2001). Trump issued many statements that primed race, as noted previously, and his campaign slogan itself was seen as potentially a racial cue, since "Make America Great Again" indicated that at some point in the past, America was a much better country. As many pointed out though, at no time in its history have blacks and other minorities been more prominent and powerful, so a revanchist slogan lends itself to a white supremacist interpretation.

Another aspect of race in recent elections is the so-called "Obama effect" (Gonino 2017). Did the election of Obama, a seminal event in America's long history of race, alter white attitudes? Several possibilities emerge. Perhaps Obama's election will cause whites to believe that racism has been largely neutralized. If a black candidate can take the highest office in the land, how strong can racial barriers be? Thus, ironically, Obama's election could lead to greater opposition to programs such as affirmative action. Another effect might be that Obama's election could promote racial understanding and increase white support for programs aimed at aiding blacks. Some studies show a small effect on white attitudes pre- and post-Obama, while others show none at all (Gonino 2017).

Another group of researchers, focusing on younger whites, found that support for Trump was linked to "white vulnerability," which they defined as "the perception that whites, through no fault of their own, are losing ground to other groups." America faces a demographic turning point that researchers have long predicted; some time around 2050, whites, for the first time in U.S. history, will be a mere plurality, rather than a majority. While most voters do not follow demographic research closely, the perception that whites are increasingly losing out to minorities is widespread, particularly among working class whites

(Gest 2016). Prior research shows white voters do respond to state level racial demographics, particularly in races that feature racially charged campaigns (Mayer 1996).

So one effect of Obama's two terms in office may be a national white backlash against blacks and other minorities (Proctor 2016). Just as the election of blacks in the Reconstruction South inflamed white resentment, trackers of radical white extremist groups claim that 2015–2016 saw a sharp rise in racial incidents. Trump's rhetoric of violence on the campaign trail, and his initial failure to disavow endorsements from Klan leaders, alt-rightists, and Neo-Nazis, is seen by some as evidence that he deliberately rode this wave of resentment, or that he played a role in its strengthening (Proctor 2016).

The "Trump as backlash to Obama" claim has been made most prominently and consistently by political scientist Michael Tesler and writer Ta-Nehisi Coates. Tesler found that Obama's presidency had increased, rather than decreased, racial polarization:

> Mass politics had become more polarized by racial attitudes since Barack Obama's rise to prominence. That is, the election of President Obama helped usher in a "most racial" political era where racially liberal and racially conservative Americans were more divided over a whole host of political positions than they had been in modern times *(Tesler 2016:3)*

Tesler's coauthored book *Identity Crisis*, written after the 2016 election, argued that race had been the prism through which many white voters interpreted their economic conditions. The unexpected support that Trump found in certain pockets of white working class communities was less about the economics than it was about white identity (Sides, Tesler, and Vavreck 2018).

Coates has made a similar argument. He directly links Trump's rise to the presidency of Obama. Coates argued that in response to the first black president, America promptly elected the first "white" president, a president who runs on white identity, and who whips up support on that basis.

The symbolic power of Barack Obama's presidency—that whiteness was no longer strong enough to prevent peons from taking up residence in the castle—assaulted the most deeply rooted notions of white supremacy and instilled fear in its adherents and beneficiaries. And it was that fear that gave the symbols Donald Trump deployed—the symbols of racism—enough potency to make him president . . . *(Coates 2017:8)*

In Trump's victory, Coates sees a reaffirmation of white power and the centrality of systemic bigotry to our politics (p. 361).

These assertions have not gone unchallenged. Musa al-Gharbi, among others, alleges that Coates and others are biased in their analyses of Trump. They ignore confounding data, such as the slight rise in black and Hispanic support for Trump as compared to Romney, or the overall drop in percent of the white electorate supporting the GOP in 2016 compared to 2012. Al-Gharbi also points out that many of these alleged racist whites voted for Obama in 2008 and/or 2012 (al-Gharbi 2018).

Still, Trump supporters were found to be particularly prone to racist attitudes in a number of studies:

A Reuters survey in June found Trump supporters were more likely than Clinton supporters to see blacks as "criminal," "unintelligent," "lazy" and "violent," though Clinton supporters were certainly not immune to those prejudices. Analysis by the RAND Corporation' Presidential Election Panel Survey found that "Trump performs best among Americans who express more resentment toward African Americans and immigrants and who tend to evaluate whites more favorably than minority groups." And even those Trump voters who did not approve of his remarks and policy proposals aimed at blacks, Muslims, and Latinos did not find them disqualifying. *(Serwer 2016)*

And Trump's rhetoric was remarkably laden with racial cues or outright racist claims. Trump's most blatantly racist act was his repeated allegation that Obama was ineligible for the presidency because he wasn't born in the United States. Neither GOP nominee in 2008 or 2012 went near this racist lie, either because they respected the truth too much or they worried that it would be seen by the media and moderate whites as prejudiced conspiracy theorizing. Trump raised the issue throughout Obama's presidency. The perception that a black man in the White House was somehow an alien presence, illegally occupying a symbol of white power, was a modern version of Reconstruction backlash, according to observers such as Coates. Just as white Southerners saw the election of black politicians and white politicians supported by blacks from 1868 to 1880 as cause for violent revolt, Trump and his followers were outraged to the point of advocating insurrection by Obama's election and re-election. On the day after Obama's re-election, Trump Tweeted this:

> We can't let this happen. We should march on Washington and stop this travesty. Our nation is totally divided!
>
> 12:29 AM - 7 Nov 2012

If the racial resentment or vulnerability of certain whites was rising during Obama's presidency, no other GOP candidate could match Trump for his hatred of the nation's first black president. None of them, not even an avatar of anti-system rhetoric such as Texas Senator Ted Cruz, called for open revolt to overturn a black man's re-election.

Research Question

We will explore these questions:

> Did racial attitudes, Southern residency, or state racial demographics affect white support for Trump in the 2016 GOP primaries? Did racial attitudes, state racial demographics, or Southern residency affect white voters in the 2016 primary and general election?

Data and Methods

Our source for data was the 2016 American National Election Study. This survey was conducted on more than four thousand Americans in the months before the election, with follow-up surveys after the election. It offers a rich set of variables with which to study this election.

Our dependent variable of greatest interest is vote among whites, both in the primaries and the general election. Those who did not vote (or intend to) and those who voted for third-party candidates, were not included. We combined those who voted early with those who expressed a preference pre-election.

We used standard control variables of income (measured on a 28-point ordinal scale), age, sex, ideology, and partisan identity.

We are interested in examining whether the white South responded to Trump differently than whites in other regions. For that reason, we included a dummy variable for Southern residence in some models. Defining the South has been a question of some debate. Some scholars use only the eleven states of the Confederacy. Others include every state defined as South by the U.S. Census, which would add Maryland, Delaware, West Virginia, Oklahoma, Kentucky, and Missouri. We emulated 538 Politics.com, which used a national survey to ask which states are considered Southern, to devise a list that included the eleven Confederate states plus Kentucky. This seemed preferable; if we are studying the effect of Southern residence on voters, living in a state widely considered to be Southern would best capture the attitude.

We devised a scale of white racial resentment based on whether whites agreed with four statements questions.

Irish, Italians, Jewish and many other minorities overcame prejudice and worked their way up. Blacks should do the same without any special favors.

Generations of slavery and discrimination have created conditions that make it difficult for blacks to work their way out of the lower class.

Over the past few years, blacks have gotten less than they deserve.

It's really a matter of some people not trying hard enough; if blacks would only try harder they could be just as well off as whites.

Respondents were asked if they Agree strongly, Agree somewhat, Neither agree nor disagree, Disagree somewhat, Disagree strongly with each statement. Obviously, the second and third point in different directions than the first and fourth. To create a composite scaled variable, we reversed the values for the middle two variables, and added the four together. This created a racial resentment variable, ranging from –8 to 8, with -8 indicating the lowest level of racial resentment and 8 the maximum.

To measure whether white vulnerability was affecting whites via state demographic values, we included census estimates of state racial demographics for whites, blacks, and Hispanics. In theory, whites who lived in states where Hispanics or blacks were larger parts of the politics and society (or in states where whites were in the aggregate a smaller proportion), might have a tendency to perceive whites to be "losing ground" more than whites in other states. Hispanic and white population variables would perhaps offer a good measure of reaction to Trump's immigration rhetoric.

We also examined attitudes on general conservatism, social issues such as abortion, and immigration, to see if Trump voters in the GOP primaries were distinctive on those questions as well.

Results

Trump voters in the primaries were not the most conservative, nor were they the most Southern. They were the most racially resentful white voters in the primaries, however. As shown on Chart 6.1, Trump voters were the most filled with anti-black attitudes. The gap with Kasich and Rubio voters was particularly large, while the one with Cruz voters was considerably smaller.

Two binary logistic regression models were created to analyze the comparative effect of various variables on white vote choice in the GOP primaries. One included Southern residence and the other did not. In both models, racial resentment was the single best predictor of support for Trump, better than sex, born-again status, ideology, income, or partisanship (partisanship was included because some independents vote in some primaries). In the model that included South, that was also shown to be an effective predictor of support for Trump, second only in strength (as measured by Wald score) to racial resentment. But the effect is negative (see Table 6.1). Trump's

Racial Resentment among White Voters in the 2016 Primary

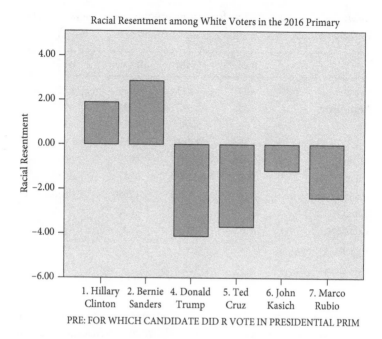

Chart 6.1. Racial resentment among white voters in the 2016 primary

support among white primary voters was weaker in the South than it was elsewhere. At the same time, racial resentment was the best predictor of Trump voting, and racial resentment among whites was far higher in the South, and to a lesser extent, in the Border States (not shown).

Trump was running in most of these primaries against two Southern candidates, Rubio and Cruz, which may help explain why Southern residence among whites was associated with a lower probability of voting for Trump compared to white residents in other regions. It may also have been the collection of cultural and political negatives listed previously, from Trump's lack of consistent faith, prior support for gun control, or simply his thick New York accent. But what we can say is that white voters in the Republican primaries seemed to have responded to his efforts to play on white racial resentment, and that that resentment was strongest in the South.

Table 6.1. Primary support for Trump among white voters—binary logistic models

	B coef	Wald	B Coef	Wald
Income	−.031*	4.843	−.030*	4.748
BornAgain	−.258	1.580	−.134	.400
Age	.004	.468	.005	.682
Sex	−.293	2.281	−59	1.754
Ideology	−.080	.568	−.077	.509
Party	.080	.126	.094	.173
Racial resentment	.115**	14.963	.125**	16.882
South			−.636**	9.260
Constant	.731	.801	.703	.725
Nagelkerke R Square		.071		.097
N		525		525

Another way of looking at Trump's primary results is by looking at how he did in the overall state totals in contested primaries and caucuses, region by region.[1] As shown on Table 6.2, Trump's strongest region was the Northeast. It is not unusual for a candidate in any election to do best in their home region. But Trump's pattern of winning the most votes in the Northeast on his way to victory mirrors that of Republicans in the most recent election cycles. Romney and McCain (in 2012 and 2008 respectively) were also strongest in the Northeast. What was unusual about Trump's victory was the remarkable national character of his primary victory; the gap between his strongest region and his weakest region was a mere 13 percent, far less than his nearest rival, and far less than the historic Republican primary norms. In a primary contest with a record number of candidates in the early stages, and an unusual number of candidates competing late in the game, Trump managed to win delegates in every region in a fairly uniform way. His victory seems less regional than many other successful Republican nominees.

Primaries, however, are not really national campaigns. The early states matter much more than later states, because early momentum attracts funding and media coverage. Trump lost Iowa and won

Table 6.2. Regional performance of GOP candidates in contested presidential primaries 1976, 2008, 2012, 2016

Region	Trump 2016	Cruz 2016	Romney 2012	Santorum 2012	McCain 2008	Huckabee 2008	Ford 1976	RR 1976
South	39	28	35	26	41	35	42	58
Border	35	36	27	46	24	39	54	45
Midwest	33	35	57	39	34	32	52	45
West	35	39	44	26	24	14	35	63
North	46	17	55	13	51	13	68	29
Largest Regional Gap	13	22	30	36	27	36	33	34

New Hampshire, making the next contest in South Carolina crucial. Trump's victory there established him firmly as the front runner. The next big test was the "SEC Primary," a collection of mostly Southern contests occurring on March 1st. Trump won every Southern contest save Cruz's home state of Texas. Trump's unbroken record of wins in the South was a key moment for his campaign. The New York sybarite had somehow used strength in the South to win the nomination.

Three binary logistic regression models were calculated for the general election: one with racial resentment, one with racial resentment and Southern residence, and one with state black population level. Again, racial resentment remains a powerful predictor of white support for Trump. In both the first and second model, it is approximately equal to partisan identity in its effect, and more powerful overall than ideology. Southern residence, however, either alone (not shown) or with racial resentment, seemed to not affect voter choice. In the third model, black population has a small, but statistically significant effect on vote between Trump and Clinton. White voters living in states with a higher percentage black were more likely to vote for Trump, even after ideology, partisanship, and the other control variables were included.[2]

Again, statewide totals seem to tell a different story, one in which the South was vitally important. If we compare Trump's regional strengths with how general election campaigns have worked for Republicans in the past, we see that Trump's strongest regions in terms of popular vote total was the South and Border South. Moreover, regional polarization in 2016 was at an all-time high. Trump badly lost the Northeast, as have most recent Republicans, and the gap between the Northeast and his best region, the Border South, was twenty-six points. Regional polarization in vote totals, as measured by the gap between the best and worst regions, has been growing since at least 2000, and Trump's election was a continuation of that trend. So, oddly enough, Republican primaries are less characterized by regionalism than ever before, but the general election looks far more regionally polarized than in recent history. This reflects the homogenization of the Republican Party. The intra-party regional divides that were legendary in the GOP primaries of 1964, 1976, and 1980 were, by 2016, almost gone. The party had adopted a very Southern conservatism on

Table 6.3. General election support for Trump among white voters—binary logistic models

	Resentment		Res+South		Black Pop	
	B coef	Wald	B Coef	Wald	B Coef	Wald
Income	-.030*	4.258	-.035*	6.114	-.032**	6.527
BornAgain	.132	.302	.394	2.810	.434*	4.043
Age	.000	.000	-.005	.711	.001	.034
Sex	-.015	.005	.083	.163	-.165	.772
Ideology	1.044**	94.933	.868**	74.977	1.204**	158.40
Party	1.686**	107.32	1.630**	101.454	1.659**	128.50
Racial resentment	.300**	93.579	.325**	109.732		
South			.326	1.802		
State Black Population					.026*	3.959
Constant	-7.498	108.56	-6.608	96.290	-7.774	146.624
Nagelkerke R Square	.81		.80		.772	
N	1484		1479		1620	

Table 6.4. Regional performance of GOP in general election by state

Republican presidential performance by region, 1980–2016, with South-Northeast gap

Region (# of states)	2016	2012	2008	2004	2000	1996 (Perot)	1992 (Perot)	1988	1984	1980
South (11)	55	55	54	57	54	46 (7)	43 (13)	59	62	50
Border (4)	63	61	57	59	55	43 (10)	38 (19)	53	61	52
Midwest (11)	52	51	48	55	53	44 (10)	39 (22)	53	60	54
West (13)	46	50	48	55	53	44 (9)	37 (24)	55	63	57
Northeast (12)	37	36	36	41	37	32 (9)	32 (19)	49	54	44
Largest Regional Gap	26	25	21	16	17	14 (12)	11 (5)	10	9	13

questions of race, taxes, defense, abortion, and nationalism. This near uniformity of approach directly contributed to the regional polarization rising in the general election.

Another way of looking at the South is to divide it, as an early chapter of this volume did, into Stagnant and Growth States. The Growth States (TX, VA, FL, GA, SC, and NC) have experienced vast economic success and population growth, along with rising diversity. The stagnant states (AL, MI, LA, AR, TN) have experienced less of all that. Chart 6.2 demonstrates that over time, Republicans have lost strength in the Growth South, and gained it in the Stagnant South. Trump experienced the greatest gap between Growth and Stagnant, doing almost ten points better in the Stagnant States, whereas in 1980, Reagan's performance in those two groups was almost indistinguishable. A somewhat similar pattern appeared in the primaries, where Trump did four points better in the Stagnant South than he did in the Growth South, the opposite of the primary performance of Romney in 2012, who did twenty-one points better in Growth States.

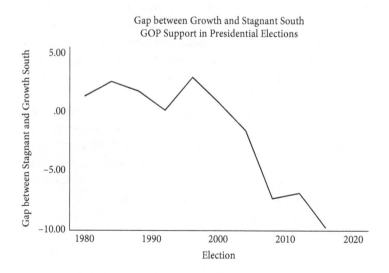

Chart 6.2. Gap between growth and stagnant South GOP support in presidential elections.

A Second Post-Reconstruction and
the Southernization of American Racial Politics?

Trump's Southern dominance was crucial to the outcome of the election. The Democrats put forth resources intending to win Florida, North Carolina, and Virginia, and at least thought about Georgia and Texas. They also spent crucial political capital on winning the South when they selected Virginia senator Tim Kaine as the vice presidential nominee. In the end, Trump did better in the South than had Romney or McCain, although not as well as Bush in 2000. By winning every Southern state except Virginia, Trump was able to eke out a narrow victory in the Midwest. But had Florida and North Carolina not gone for Trump, Hillary would have won the presidency while losing Pennsylvania, Wisconsin, and Michigan. A similar argument could be made about the Republican primaries. Had Trump not done better in state victories in the South than he did in any other region (only losing one state), he might well have seen the anti-Trump establishment coalesce around Cruz or Rubio in time to deny him the nomination.

In short, the South mattered a great deal in 2016, despite all the attention to the Democrats' failed Blue Wall in the Rust Belt states. But the best evidence of the South mattering came much earlier in the form of the set of issue positions that Trump called his agenda. Trump has almost no committed political views or ideology. The only major issues that he hasn't budged on since his first flirtation with the presidency in 1988 are free trade (he's opposed), law and order, nationalism, and white resentment (Kruse 2016). Everything else has been malleable. He's been radically pro-choice, pro-gun control, for universal healthcare, even for aggressive new taxes on wealth (West 2018). Yet as he prepared for his 2016 campaign, he adopted the policy preferences of a Southern conservative Republican. Extreme support for gun rights, extreme anti-abortion (even advocating punishment for women who attempt to get abortions), and pretending to revere the Bible. Just as hypocrisy is the tribute vice pays to virtue, when a rudderless political figure adopts certain positions in lockstep with a movement or region, it is proof of its power. It is no accident that the first major endorser of Trump in the GOP was a Deep South Southerner from the Stagnant State of Alabama.

The data we examine here suggest that Trump's racial rhetoric, racial past, or racial meaning was perceived and had an impact on both the primary and general election. In the primary, the Southern Republican electorate did not embrace Trump as strongly as whites did elsewhere. But he also won a higher percentage of Southern primaries than he did in any other region. As discussed previously, Southern whites overlooked all of Trump's defects as a candidate in the South. While our data cannot allow us to conclude with certainty that they did so because of his racial/ethnic rhetoric, it certainly seems plausible. However, as noted in the opening section, given the number of ways in which Trump was sui generis, and the number of factors unique to the 2016 election, it remains possible the white South was responding to one of them, or some combination of them. It could even be that some white Southerners were reluctant to support Trump because he was so bluntly racial.

Still, racial resentment was among the most powerful predictors of white vote in both elections. Is this one version of an "Obama effect" in which some whites no longer believe that blacks have any need for government programs or excuses since a black man won the presidency? Or is it evidence of a white backlash against some kind of second Reconstruction? Again, our data cannot allow us to affirmatively answer either of those questions. What we can say is that racial attitudes remain remarkably important in American elections. In this, we are largely in agreement with the prior research of Tesler and others. Race was a fulcrum that moved much of the politics of 2016.

The electoral impact of black population level in the general election, while small, is not only statistically significant but worth discussing separately. Why do some whites respond to black population? It is of course possible that the effect is actually among white voters in lower black population states. Perhaps those whites are more open to voting Democratic because they don't associate the Democratic Party as strongly with blacks as do whites in states where blacks are more prominent in the political world. Maybe whites in Vermont or Wyoming feel the opposite of "white vulnerability"—some form of "white confidence" with the state demographics that allows more voting for the party of Obama. But black population levels, which used to shape white voting patterns in the Southern region, can now be shown to influence white voting behavior nationally.[3]

In the final analysis, the results here suggest that Trump's remarkable embrace of racist tropes such as "Obama was born in Kenya," "blacks have it better than whites today," and "Black Lives Matter is a terrorist organization" affected white voting patterns nationwide. His primary victories in the South show that that region found something special in Trump. Indeed, the whites of the South supported Trump in the primaries strongly. The New York sybarite, whose personal history, religious values, and prior political positions should have made the South the graveyard of his political ambitions, was instead embraced by Southern white Republicans in the primary and general elections. Given the strong link between voting for Trump and resentment of blacks, Trump's blunt anti-black rhetoric and white nationalist nativism are the most likely explanations.

In that sense, perhaps the 2016 election is further evidence of the normalization of the South, or indeed the Southernization of American politics. The white South remains the most resentful of blacks, according to the data we examined and many other studies. But it is not nearly as much of an outlier on racial attitudes as it once was. That change may also be because in a very unexpected way, national politics have become more Southern. The American system has faced no greater challenge in the last forty years than polarization. That polarization is almost as stark on racial lines as it is on partisan ones. Blacks are almost nonexistent in the Republican Party, as are most other minorities. The Trump coalition was a stubbornly white one, even after years of GOP plans to enlarge their minority support. That pattern, of racial polarization, in which one party speaks for one race and the other speaks for those who resent that race, was the Southern party system during and immediately after Reconstruction. The meaning of the 2016 election of Donald J. Trump is, among other things, a confirmation that national politics has become more deeply polarized by race, in a way that can be seen as an echo of that Southern political history.

7

Conclusion

The South of today bears little resemblance to a half century ago. More telling though, as the preceding chapters show, is how rapidly and profoundly the South has changed in recent years. The region, a stronghold of the Republican Party at the federal, state, and local levels since the 1990s, has moved increasingly into a competitive partisan position as Virginia has turned Democratic dominated and several other states (particularly Florida, Georgia, North Carolina, and even Texas somewhat) have become two-party battlegrounds. GOP support in the South now is largely relegated to white voters—mostly men and generally middle-aged and older—who comprise a declining percentage of the region's population.

For those who believe that demographics are destiny, the future appears bright for the Democratic Party in the region. Minority and younger voters, the bulwark of the party, are expanding their ranks in the South rapidly. Underlying such analysis though is the assumption that current population trends will continue unabated and that voting preferences among groups will remain static. It is conceivable that voting preferences of groups could change, depending on varied factors that drive voters to one party or the other. In the Trump era it may seem highly improbable, for example, that Latino voters, the fastest growing segment of the population in the South, will switch loyalties to the Republican Party. But prior to Trump's presidency, a good many Republican candidates for office in the South, including President George W. Bush, fared quite well with Latino voters. It is entirely possible that post-Trump, the GOP will embrace an open, inclusive message that appeals to growing segments of the population.

Thus, predicting the future of the politics of the South is fraught with challenges, as is the case with all political predicting. Who thought fifty years ago that the "solid South" of Democratic Party domination would become by the 1990s the most reliably Republican region of the country that anchored the party's national fortunes? Or, in the 1990s very few foresaw the evolution of a near solidly Republican South becoming increasingly friendly to Democratic Party messages and candidates.

The preceding chapters have described and analyzed the key factors that explain Southern political transformation of the past half century and point the way toward further analysis of how these factors likely will affect the politics and governance of the region and nationally.

Changing Demographics: The South has had the greatest population growth of any region of the country in the past half century, with the most explosive growth coming from Florida, Texas, and Georgia. Those states are followed by North Carolina, South Carolina, and Virginia. The population growth of these states, driven largely by in-migration from other states, but also internationally, is largely attributable to economic and social dynamism.

With this high population growth has come a vast change in the makeup of the region's demographics. A half century ago the South had a biracial makeup of whites and blacks who mostly lived in the states in which they were born. In 1970, the South was about three-quarters non-Hispanic white and about 20 percent black. The influx of newcomers of all ages, races, ethnicities, and occupations has given the South a vastly different look, driven substantially by in-migration of Latinos and to a lesser extent Asians. The increasing number of interracial marriages and thus persons with mixed ancestry has also redefined the composition of the Southern population, whereas barely more than a half century ago such marriages were illegal in the Southern states. Today the Southern population is about 55 percent non-Hispanic white, 20 percent Hispanic, and 19 percent black.

Future population growth in the South will be driven largely by minority groups. Not only in-migration from other states and countries, but also relatively higher birth rates among minorities than non-Hispanic whites are making the South increasingly diverse. The foreign-born component of the population is more than 10 percent now in four Southern states, and 14 percent in the region overall, and increasing fast in the higher population growth Southern states. In six

Southern states domestic net migration (more people moving in than moving out) is outpacing in-migration from other countries.

Demographic changes in the region have meant larger numbers of minorities and women elected to public offices, increasingly competitive two-party politics, and more political polarization by race, place of birth, age, education, income, and gender. Changes in the Southern population have thus had major impacts on national politics and governing. Republicans had increasingly looked south to anchor their national political fortunes, but today with greater diversification of the population regionally the pendulum has begun swinging toward the Democrats. Yet, some evidence suggests increasing numbers of Southern voters, especially the younger adults, willing to shun both political parties. Thus, whatever current demographic trends suggest today about the future of politics in the South may not hold into the future.

Changing Partisanship: For generations many assumed that Democratic hegemony in the South would last forever. The old "Solid South" lasted longer than the life of the Soviet Union and of the rule of the house of Stuart in Britain. During this era the South had been banished from occupying the White House—there was no Southern president from 1849 to 1963—and it played only a minor role in the selection of chief executives.

By the 1970s though, the South became a crucial battleground in the election of the president, and the region became the home of presidents elected in 1976, 1988, 1992, 1996, 2000, and 2004. As the Democratic Party became the party of civil rights and increasingly anchored by minority voters, the South became two-party competitive with many conservative Democrats switching their loyalties to the GOP. Beginning with the Reagan era, numerous Democratic elected officials in the South, including members of Congress, switched parties. The more the national Democratic Party swung to the left, the more Southern Democrats realigned to the GOP, creating ultimately a highly polarized region politically. The South today elects many of the most conservative Republicans to Congress and their influence has moved the legislative caucus nationally to the far right.

Republican gains in the South began at the presidential level in the 1950s and slowly trickled down to statewide elections and much later

Although the process took decades to complete, by the dominance of the region began to look like an emerging as two Southern Democrats occupied the White House. The realignment of the Southern electorate by then was in full force and by the 2000s, with the election and re-election to the presidency of a Texan, the GOP sweep of the South looked complete.

As the GOP crested in the South, Democrats began to make important comebacks in the region, led by Virginia. Although the Old Dominion had voted GOP in every presidential race from 1952 to 2004, excepting the 1964 Lyndon Baines Johnson landslide, it has now gone Democratic in three consecutive presidential elections, and no Republican has won any statewide office since 2009. The last Republican elected to the U.S. Senate from Virginia won in 2002. Democratic candidates have become very competitive statewide recently in North Carolina, Georgia, Florida, and Texas. These five states hold out the prospect of anchoring a future Southern political realignment toward the Democratic Party.

The Changing Politics of Race: A little more than a half century ago the Voting Rights Act (VRA) wiped away the barriers to black voter registration and voting that had kept blacks from the voting booth in the South for generations. Prior to the VRA, merely 43 percent of the black adult population in the region was registered to vote. By 1970, two-thirds of the region's eligible black population had registered. In some states the change was dramatic, as black registration in this period in Mississippi, for example, increased from 7 to 60 percent.

The long era of racial segregation and black voter suppression coincided with the old "Solid South" of Democratic dominance of the region. Among African Americans who could vote, they were loyal to the GOP, the party of Lincoln. The VRA and the civil rights movement more generally moved Southern blacks to the Democratic Party. The emergence of African American voters' rights and their realigning to the Democratic Party have had the most profound impact on the politics of the region of the past half century.

Today, remarkably Southern African Americans vote at about the same rate as whites and in some recent presidential elections have exceeded white participation. As whites realigned to the GOP, African Americans became a key component of the Democratic

Party dominance of the South, with substantial influence on legislative priorities. As the GOP gained ascendancy in the region though, African American influence dwindled in the state legislatures, even as more African Americans were winning seats. Redistricting furthered this trend, as majority-minority districts promoted African American electoral success while simultaneously reducing minority voter influence in surrounding districts, thereby facilitating Republican success in these districts.

Race drives much of the political polarization of the region. African Americans are the core constituency of the Democratic Party and white Evangelicals are the most loyal Republicans. Black support for Democrats is nearly cohesive, whereas white Evangelical support for Republicans is overwhelming and often offsets support for Democrats. As the Southern electorate becomes less white, the Democratic Party seems positioned to gain ground in the region.

The Changing Politics of Religion: The rise of the largely Evangelical-led Christian Right movement profoundly altered the Southern political landscape and eventually nationally as well. About a half century ago the presidential campaign GOP nominee Richard M. Nixon reached out to Southern evangelicals in an effort to break the Democratic Party dominance of the region. The third-party presidential candidacy of native son Southerner George Wallace limited GOP gains with Evangelicals that year, but not long after the Christian Right mobilized politically due to what it considered in the 1970s a fast-paced growing national tolerance of abortion, gay rights, and restrictions on public expressions of Christian faith.

The 1976 presidential candidacy of another southern native son, Democrat Jimmy Carter, delayed the eventual GOP capture of Southern Evangelical voters. An openly born-again Christian, Carter attracted substantial support from faith-based voters and he swept all but one of the Southern states (Virginia) in his close victory over President Gerald R. Ford. Carter's victory demonstrated the power of the Southern Evangelical and born-again vote, and Republican strategists took note.

In 1980, GOP presidential candidate Ronald Reagan seized on Evangelical voters' disappointment with Carter's liberal social policy agenda to attract their support. The Lynchburg, Virginia, Rev. Jerry

Falwell's Christian Right group Moral Majority had formed in 1979 to help attract Evangelicals to the GOP and he claimed credit for having brought millions of previously apolitical born-again believers who had supported Carter into the Republican Party in 1980. The GOP landslide that year seemed to confirm that the Christian Right had played a big role in the GOP's successes and Falwell himself became an instant nationally prominent political figure. An emboldened Christian Right landed firmly in the GOP and has been the most reliable constituency since. The Moral Majority gave way to the Christian Coalition, also headquartered in Virginia, and that group has given way to a myriad of social conservative groups and networks that exert major influence on GOP nominations, platforms, elections, and public policies primarily in the Southern states, but nationally as well now.

The rise of the Christian Right played a major role in reconfiguring first the Southern political landscape before spreading across much of the nation. The "Solid South," long a predominantly white Protestant and Democratic Party dominated region has become largely Republican, anchored by white Protestants. As the South has become increasingly diverse and somewhat less distinctive, coalitions of minority groups, including religious minorities, are the backbone of the Democratic Party in the region. Since the 1980s, white Evangelicals have remained firmly committed to the GOP. Even in presidential elections that favored the Democrats in the popular vote (1992, 1996, 2000, 2008, 2012, 2016), the Republicans' Evangelical base in the South has remained solid. Some Democratic Party candidates in the South have reached out to Evangelicals but to date there is little evidence that those voters are open to such appeals.

The Changing Politics of the Trump Era

To most political observers in early 2016, GOP presidential candidate Donald J. Trump was not credible running in the South. He had no regional affinity with the South and no religious background. Moreover, his multiple marriages, very public affairs, thick New York accent, and often crude language, made him seem to many as antithetical to Southern GOP voters. Finally, the South had long been unfriendly territory in the party primaries to presidential aspirants from the Northeast. Nonetheless, the South has been the most conservative voting region in the nation in the presidential primaries of both political parties, and Trump ran hard-right, particularly on hot button issues such as immigration, gun rights, and abortion. In a highly crowded GOP field, Trump differentiated himself enough to gain the support necessary to march to his unlikely nomination. His even more unlikely general election win followed, relied on the near-sweep of the South fueled by fervent white Evangelical support.

Trump's election as president with strong Southern support underscores the effects of the critical transformations in Southern politics described in the previous chapters. His continued success in 2020 may depend heavily on whether the hints of a Democratic resurgence in the region's Growth States come to fruition.

Despite the region's growing diversity, the attendant polarization of the electorate has emboldened the still numerically dominant white population that remains solidly Republican. Minority voter turnout in the region and nationally spiked with Barack Obama leading the presidential ticket in 2008 and 2012. Hillary Clinton in 2016 inspired far less enthusiasm. To pry Southern states from their GOP anchorage will require African American participation at Obama election rates along with critical support from Hispanic and Asian communities.

Race clearly was a motivating factor in the 2016 elections, as Trump led the "birthers" in challenging the legitimacy of Barack Obama's citizenship. To many African Americans and others, this claim seemed heavily tinged with racism. Trump's claims appealed to white racial resentment over a black man in the Oval Office and, ugly as it was, this tactic earned Trump a following as he plotted his run for the presidency. Trump's presidential campaign announcement in which he made inflammatory comments about immigrants from Mexico fueled more charges that he was making racially based appeals. Data show that among all of the GOP presidential aspirants, Trump's voters were indeed the most racially resentful whites, and white racial resentment was strongest in the Southern primaries. Trump won the critical South Carolina primary after losing Iowa and New Hampshire. In the March 1, 2016, "SEC Primary" of mostly Southern states, Trump won every Southern contest except Texas, which he lost to native son senator Ted Cruz. In the general election Trump's strongest regions were the South and then the Border South states. Regional polarization was particularly strong in 2016, with the gap between GOP and Democratic voting regions being vast.

Religion finally was a key variable in Trump's election, as he polled 81 percent of the white Evangelical vote—a larger percentage than achieved by more authentically religious conservative candidates Mitt Romney and George W. Bush, and better than John McCain, George H. W. Bush, and Ronald Reagan. As most observers focused on Trump's highly unlikely victories in key Midwest and Upper Midwest states in the Electoral College, his near sweep of the South anchored by white Evangelicals was in some ways even more critical to his election.

Final Words

When two of us in the 1990s embarked on an edited collection of scholarly papers on the changing politics of the Southern states, our editor casually suggested that the book would have a short lifespan given that the South would not long remain distinctive or worthy of continued study. His belief in the homogenization of American politics over time was not unusual, and today there are claims that the South is losing, or has completely lost, its distinctiveness. Two decades after our volume appeared, our same editor welcomed the sixth edition of the book (Bullock and Rozell, eds., 2018). Interest in the politics of the South remains strong because of its continued relevance as a distinctive region of the country, though not always distinctive for the same reasons as it was a half century ago.

Demographic changes in the region indeed have made the South look a bit more like much of the rest of the United States. Increasing partisan competition in some parts of the region show a different South than the one long dominated by a single party. Racial progress in the region too cannot be denied. And the rise of Evangelical political activism, first centered in the South, has spread to large parts of the United States. And yet, there are forces in place, especially the intensified polarization of the country, that make analyses of a distinctive South necessary. Furthermore, as the chapters here showcase, the differences within the South between the High Growth, Moderate Growth, and Stagnant States explain much about the within-region distinctions that characterize Southern politics.

As we close this volume, President Trump is barely at the halfway point of his term in office and, despite a tumultuous two years at the job, he retains very strong support in much of the South and appears to be building a re-election strategy around his Southern base. With the polarization of the country so intense, much speculation surrounds whether the Democratic Party will, in reaction to Trump, turn far left in its presidential nominating contest, which likely would further exacerbate the regional chasms in the electorate. Whatever the outcome, the direction of U.S. national politics and governing will continue to be driven substantially by what happens in the South.

Notes

Chapter 1

1. The precise line came from Wallace's gubernatorial inaugural address given on January 14, 1963, but captured the philosophy on which he campaigned for president.
2. One Texas African American, Will Hurd, is a Republican.
3. Alabama, Georgia, Louisiana, Mississippi, and South Carolina constitute the Deep South. The Rim South consists of Arkansas, Florida, North Carolina, Tennessee, Texas, and Virginia.
4. With one exception, the date in Table 1.5 is when the Republican Party wins and maintains a majority. The one exception occurs in Virginia's congressional delegation where Republicans' majority status was maintained from 1999 until 2019 with the exception of 1999–2000. The loss of three House seats in 2018 reduced the GOP delegation to four and is in keeping with Democratic resurgence in the state that has seen Democrats control all of the statewide offices and come within two seats of a majority in the lower chamber of the state legislature.

Chapter 2

1. The 1970 Census did not directly ask about Hispanic origin. The figures here are based on an imputation of Hispanic origin based on Spanish language. Whites are only non-Hispanic, while blacks include the Hispanic portion of that population. Hispanics are of any race. For more information and source data, see Gibson and Jung (2002). In the 2017 figures, whites, blacks, and Asians include only single-race non-Hispanics. Hispanics are of any race. The 2017 figures are from U.S. Census Bureau. 2018. Table B03002 Hispanic or Latino Origin by Race, 2017 American Community Survey 1-year estimates.

2. Author's analysis of 1994 and 2017 IPUMS Current Population Survey microdata (Flood et al., 2018).

Chapter 3

1. Woodrow Wilson had Southern roots and attitudes about race but most of his adult life and all of his political experience came in the North where he served as governor of New Jersey.
2. The Rim or Peripheral States are Arkansas, Florida, North Carolina, Tennessee, Texas, and Virginia. Alabama, Georgia, Louisiana, Mississippi, and South Carolina constitute the Deep South.
3. The coattails strategy proved unavailing as no additional Republicans got elected from the South and the GOP lost a Virginia seat it had held since 1953.
4. During the 1950s, Republicans won a total of thirty House contests in the South, with eight the most in any election year.
5. Black Republicans, many of whom were disfranchised due to various practices, largely left the GOP at about the time of the Goldwater candidacy.
6. North Carolina also has partisan registration but we have been unable to find figures on the racial composition of party members.
7. This was part of the Dream Team that slated former Dallas mayor Ron Kirk for the Senate, Tony Sanchez for governor, and John Sharp for lieutenant governor. The hope that having at the top of the ticket an African American, a Hispanic, and an Anglo would lead to victory went unfulfilled.
8. Two of the white Democrats from Texas did not seek re-election in 2018 as one retired and the other ran for the Senate. Both of these individuals represented majority-Hispanic districts.
9. From 1899 when Oscar Underwood (AL) became the first Democratic whip until 1971, a Southerner filled the office for thirty-nine years; a Border state member served sixteen years; from 1909 to 1913, the position was vacant; and a Northerner served thirteen years.
10. In 1969, Linwood Holton won Virginia's governorship. He was succeeded by Mills Godwin (R) in 1973, and in 1977 John Dalton (R) became the third Republican governor in a row. Virginia is now the only state that does not allow a governor to serve even a second consecutive term.
11. The 2014 Georgia ticket also had the advantage of names well known to the state's voters. Carter is the grandson of President Carter, and Nunn sought the Senate seat held by her father for four terms (1972–1997).

12. In 2000, George Bush won 43 percent of the Texas Hispanic vote. In his 2004 re-election, he got 49 percent.

13. Currently Alabama, Arkansas, Georgia, Mississippi, South Carolina, and Texas require a majority for nomination while North Carolina has a 40-percent threshold. Until 2002 Florida also had a majority-vote requirement, and North Carolina demanded a majority until 1989.

14. The South Carolina situation was complex. The winner of the runoff, Pug Ravenel, was disqualified for not meeting the residency requirement having only recently returned from New York. The state party substituted the loser of the runoff, William Jennings Bryan Dorn, a decision to which Ravenel never became reconciled.

15. Florida does not stage separate contests for lieutenant governor. Candidates for governor and lieutenant governor run as a team.

Chapter 4

1. The career of George Wallace demonstrates this shift. Upon losing his first bid to become governor of Alabama in the 1958 when he ran as a populist but lost to the race-baiting John Patterson, Wallace vowed, "no other son-of-a-bitch will ever out-nigger me again" (Carter 1995, 96). A generation later in his last bid for office, Wallace, who had publicly repented his own racist campaigns, depended on black votes, of which he got as much as 90 percent, to defeat Montgomery mayor Emory Folmar (Tullos 2011).

2. An African American represented Tennessee's Memphis district for thirty-two years until Steven Cohen won the decisive Democratic primary with 31 percent of the vote when more than a dozen African American contenders split the black vote.

3. Justices on a state's Supreme Court are often elected statewide, but not always. In Louisiana and Mississippi justices are elected from districts while justices are chosen by the legislature in South Carolina and Virginia.

4. Georgia and South Carolina are the two states that regularly report racial breakdowns for the party primary

5. Pursuant to the 1965 VRA, Alabama, Georgia, Louisiana, Mississippi, South Carolina, Virginia, and about half of North Carolina had to have any changes in laws having any impact on politics approved either by the Department of Justice or the federal district court sitting in Washington, DC, prior to implementation. The 1975 VRA extended pre-clearance to Texas and five Florida counties.

6. For a review of the various estimates of the number of districts gained by the GOP as a result of the creation of majority-black districts, see Lublin (1997, 111–114). Figures range from zero to seventeen.

7. *Reno v. Bossier Parish School Board,* 528 U.S. 320 (2000).

8. See *Shaw v. Reno,* 509 U.S. 630 (1993); *Miller v. Johnson,* 515 U.S. 900 (1995); *Bush v. Vera,* 517 U.S. 952 (1996).

9. Of course, nothing is permanent in politics. But Republicans have retained their majorities in the South Carolina House and Florida Senate since the 1994 takeovers. Partisan control of the North Carolina House seesawed back and forth until 2010; currently Republicans are in their third consecutive term as the majority. The word "permanent" is used to distinguish from the one term when Republicans organized the Tennessee House in the 1960s.

10. In some chambers, such as in Georgia's Senate and both the Texas House and Senate, members of the minority party get to lead a few committees, often among the least active. In those situations, a few African Americans have chaired committees.

11. Currently no Democrats hold statewide offices in Alabama, Georgia, South Carolina, Tennessee, or Texas.

12. A similar challenge has questioned Hispanic concentrations in some Texas districts.

13. Texas no longer has a majority white population, but when its citizens go to the polls, most voters remain white.

Chapter 5

1. Jimmy Carter's presidential campaign of 1976 is notable given that he was a "born-again" Christian from the South and garnered much support from Evangelical Christians, but Carter merely delayed the Christian Right's movement toward the GOP. Carter did prove, however, that conservative Christians could be mobilized politically.

Chapter 6

1. In this section, South is defined as only the eleven states of the Confederacy, with a new category, Border States, for Missouri, Kentucky, West Virginia, and Oklahoma.

2. No such effect was found for Hispanic population or white population.

3. The dogs that did not bark in our data, overall white population and Hispanic population, suggest that if whites are concerned about immigration and the relative proportion of whites, they are doing so more in response to national messages and national demographics, rather than state. Or, perhaps the lack of effect is because while Hispanics are the largest minority, nationally and in many states, they remain less politically powerful than African Americans, and less powerful than their potential, for a number of reasons such as citizenship concerns, low voter turnout, and political culture. Hispanics also tend to identify as whites racially, and Hispanics ethnically, and so some whites may perceive Hispanics dynamically, similar to how whites gradually admitted Irish and Italians into whiteness over decades (Ignatiev 2012).

References

al-Gharbi, Musa. 2018. "Race and the Race for the White House: On Social Research in the Age of Trump." *The American Sociologist* 49, no. 4: 496–519.

Alter, Charlotte. 2018. "How Women Candidates Changed American Politics in 2018." *Time*, November 7, 2018. http://time.com/5446556/congress-women-pink-wave/ (last accessed by author on February 2, 2019).

Anderson, Monica, and Gustavo López. 2018. "Key Facts about Black Immigrants in the U.S." *Pew Research Center*, January 24, 2018. http://www.pewresearch.org/fact-tank/2018/01/24/key-facts-about-black-immigrants-in-the-u-s/. (last accessed by author on February 2, 2019).

Ansolabehere, Stephen. 2009. "Effects of Identification Requirements on Voting: Evidence from the Experiences of Voters on Election Day." *PS* (January): 127–130.

Ballentine, Summer. 2016. "10 States Still Haven't Elected a Minority Nonjudicial Candidate Statewide." *Associated Press*, September 3, 2016. https://www.stripes.com/news/us/10-states-still-haven-t-elected-a-minority-nonjudicial-candidate-statewide-1.427043. (last accessed by author on February 2, 2019).

Barone, Michael, and Grant Ujifusa. 1987. *The Almanac of American Politics, 1988.* Washington, DC: National Journal.

Barone, Michael, and Grant Ujifusa. 1993. *The Almanac of American Politics, 1994.* Washington, DC: National Journal.

Bass, Jack, and Walter de Vries. 1977. *The Transformation of Southern Politics: Social Change and Political Consequence since 1945.* New York: Meridian.

Basu, Tanya. 2015. "How the Past 50 Years of Immigration Changed America." *Time*, September 28, 2015. http://time.com/4050914/1965-immigration-act-pew/ (last accessed by author on February 2, 2019).

Bertrand, Marianne, and Sendhil Mullainathan. 2004. "Are Emily and Greg More Employable than Lakisha and Jamal? A Field Experiment on Labor Market Discrimination." *American Economic Review* 94, no. 4 (September): 991–1013.

Black, Earl, and Merle Black. 1989. *Politics and Society in the South.* Cambridge, MA: Harvard University Press.

Black, Earl, and Merle Black. 2002. *The Rise of Southern Republicans.* Cambridge, MA: Belknap Press of Harvard University Press.

Bobo, Lawrence. 1998. "Race, Interests, and Beliefs about Affirmative Action. *The American Behavioral Scientist* 41:985–1003.

Brady, David W., and Charles S. Bullock, III. 1980. "Is There a Conservative Coalition in the House?" *Journal of Politics* 42 (May): 549–559.

Brady, David W., and Charles S. Bullock, III. 1981. "Coalition Politics in the House of Representatives." In *Congress Reconsidered*, 2nd ed., ed. Lawrence C. Dodd and Bruce I. Oppenheimer (Washington, DC: Congressional Quarterly Press): 186–203.

Brownstein, Ronald. 2015. "The Kaleidoscope Society." *The Atlantic*, July 1, 2015. https://www.theatlantic.com/politics/archive/2015/07/the-kaleidoscope-society/432237/. (last accessed by author on February 2, 2019).

Bullock, Charles S., III. 1981. "Congressional Voting and Immobilization of a Black Electorate in the South." *Journal of Politics* 43 (August): 662–682.

Bullock, Charles S., III. 1988. "Creeping Realignment in the South." In *The South's New Politics: Realignment and Dealignment*, ed. Robert H. Swansborough and David M. Brodsky. Columbia: University of South Carolina Press.

Bullock, Charles S., III. 2003. "It's a Sonny Day in Georgia." In *Midterm Madness: The Elections of 2002*, ed. Larry J. Sabato. Lanham, MD: Rowman and Littlefield: 177–186.

Bullock, Charles S., III. 2010. "Barack Obama and the South." *American Review of Politics* 31 (Spring): 3–24.

Bullock, Charles S., III. 2014. "Georgia: Republicans at the High Water Mark?" In *The New Politics of the Old South*, 5th ed., ed. Charles S. Bullock, III, and Mark J. Rozell. Lanham, MD: Rowman and Littlefield: 49–70.

Bullock, Charles S., III, Donna R. Hoffman, and Ronald Keith Gaddie. 2005. "The Consolidation of the White Southern Congressional Vote." *Political Research Quarterly* 58 (June): 231–43.

Bullock, Charles S., III, and Daniel Kanso. 2015. "Decades of Democratic Dominance," presented at the annual meeting of the Georgia Political Science Association, Savannah, GA, November 12–14.

Bullock, Charles S., III, and Daniel Kanso. 2016. "Breakthrough: South Carolina Elects a Republican Governor," presented at the Citadel Symposium on Southern Politics, Charleston, SC, March 3–4.

Bullock, Charles S. III. 2018. "Introduction: Southern Politics in the Twenty-First Century." In *The New Politics of the Old South: An Introduction to Southern Politics,* 6th ed., ed. Charles S. Bullock III and Mark J. Rozell. Lanham, MD: Rowman and Littlefield: 1–23.

Bullock, Charles S., III, Donna R. Hoffman, and Ronald Keith Gaddie. 2006. "Regional Variations in the Realignment of American Politics, 1944–2004." *Social Science Quarterly* 87 (September): 494–518.

Bullock, Charles S., III, and Mark J, Rozell, eds., 2018. *The New Politics of the Old South: An Introduction to Southern Politics,* 6th ed.. Lanham, MD: Rowman & Littlefield.

Bullock, Charles S., III, Scott E. Buchanan, and Ronald Keith Gaddie. 2015. *The Three Governors' Controversy: Skullduggery, Machinations and the Decline of Progressive Politics in the Peach State.* Athens: University of Georgia Press.

Bullock, Charles S., III, and Ronald Keith Gaddie. 2009. *The Triumph of Voting Rights in the South.* Norman: University of Oklahoma Press.

Button, James W. 1989. *Blacks and Social Change.* Princeton, NJ: Princeton University Press.

Cameron, Charles, David Epstein, and Sharyn O'Halloran. 1996. "Do Majority-Minority Districts Maximize Black Substantive Representation in Congress?" *American Political Science Review* 90 (December): 794–812.

Carter, Dan. T. 1995 and 2000. *The Politics of Rage" George Wallace, the Origins of the New Conservativism, and the Transformation of American Politics.* New York: Simon and Schuster.

Center for American Women and Politics. 2018a. "Women in Statewide Office 2018." http://www.cawp.rutgers.edu/women-statewide-elective-executive-office-2018. (last accessed by author on February 2, 2019).

Center for American Women and Politics. 2018b. "Women in the U.S. House 2018." http://www.cawp.rutgers.edu/women-us-house-representatives-2018. (last accessed by author on February 2, 2019).

Center for American Women and Politics. 2018c. "Women of Color in Elective Office 2018." http://cawp.rutgers.edu/women-color-elective-office-2018. (last accessed by author on February 2, 2019).

Chetty, Raj, Nathaniel Hendren, Patrick Kline, and Emmanuel Saez. 2014. "Where Is the Land of Opportunity? The Geography of Intergenerational Mobility in the United States." *Quarterly Journal of Economics* 129, no. 4 (November): 1553–1623.

Coates, Ta-Nehisi. 2017. *We Were Eight Years in Power: An American Tragedy.* New York: One World.

Cohen, Martin, David Karol, Hans Noel, and John Zaller. 2008. *The Party Decides: Presidential Nominations before and after Reform.* Chicago: University of Chicago Press.

Cohn, D'Vera, and Andrea Caumont. 2016. "10 Demographic Trends That Are Shaping the U.S. and the World." *Pew Research Center*, March 31, 2016. http://www.pewresearch.org/fact-tank/2016/03/31/10-demographic-trends-that-are-shaping-the-u-s-and-the-world/. (last accessed by author on February 2, 2019).

Cohn, D'Vera, Jeffrey S. Passel, and Ana Gonzalez-Barrera. 2017. "Rise in U.S. Immigrants from El Salvador, Guatemala and Honduras Outpaces Growth from Elsewhere." *Pew Research Center.* December 7, 2017. http://www.pewhispanic.org/2017/12/07/rise-in-u-s-immigrants-from-el-salvador-guatemala-and-honduras-outpaces-growth-from-elsewhere/. (last accessed by author on February 2, 2019).

Cook, Lindsey. 2015. "Red-State Bible-Thumpers Don't Want to Live Next to Blue-State Hippies." *U.S. News & World Report*, August 14, 2015. https://www.usnews.com/news/blogs/data-mine/2015/08/14/politics-can-play-a-role-in-where-people-live-study-says. (last accessed by author on February 2, 2019).

Copenhaver, Megan. 2016. "Year in Review: Atlanta's Corporate Relocations in 2016." *Know Atlanta.* https://www.knowatlanta.com/business/year-review-atlantas-corporate-relocations-2016/. (last accessed by author on February 2, 2019).

Cosman, Bernard. 1966. *Five States for Goldwater: Continuity and Change in Southern Presidential Voting Patterns.* Tuscaloosa: University of Alabama Press.

Diment, Dmitry, Rory Masterson, and Darryle Ulama. 2016. "Economic Clusters of Western and Southern United States." *IBISWorld*, March 31, 2016. https://www.ibisworld.com/industry-insider/industry-insights/economic-clusters-of-western-and-southern-united-states/. (last accessed by author on February 2, 2019).

Dixon, John, Kevin Durrheim, and Colin Tredoux. 2007. "Inter-group Contact and Attitudes: Toward the Principle and Practice of Racial Equality." *Psychological Science* 18:67–72.

Downs, Anthony. 1957. *An Economic Theory of Democracy.* New York: Harper.

The Economist. 2008. "The Big Sort: Political Segregation." June 19, 2008. https://www.economist.com/united-states/2008/06/19/the-big-sort. (last accessed by author on February 2, 2019).

The Economist. 2016. "Pushback." March 5. https://www.economist.com/news/books-and-arts/21693910-2016-campaign-putting-most-influential-political-science-book-recent-memory (last accessed by author on February 2, 2019).

Epstein, David. 2002. Extra Report in *Georgia v. Ashcroft*, 195 F. Supp. 2d 25 (D.D.C.).

Epstein, David, and Sharyn O'Halloran. 1993. "A Social Science Approach to Race, Redistricting, and Representation." *American Political Science Review* 93 (March): 187–191.

Faigley, Lester L. 1975. "What Happened in Kanawha County." *English Journal* 64, no. 5: 7–9.

Feldman, Glenn, ed. 2005. *Politics and Religion in the White South.* Lexington: University of Kentucky Press.

Fenno, Richard F., Jr. 1996. *Senators on the Campaign Trail: The Politics of Representation.* Norman: University of Oklahoma Press.

Flood, Sarah, Miriam King, Renae Rodgers, Steven Ruggles, and J. Robert Warren. 2018. Integrated Public Use Microdata Series, Current Population Survey: Version 6.0 [dataset]. Minneapolis, MN: IPUMS, 2018. https://doi.org/10.18128/D030.V6.0. (last accessed by author on February 2, 2019).

Fouriezos, Nick. 2018. "The Key to 2018? Asian-Americans in the Suburbs." *OZY*, March 14, 2018. https://www.ozy.com/politics-and-power/the-key-to-2018-asian-americans-in-the-suburbs/83788. (last accessed by author on February 2, 2019).

Fowler, Matthew, Vladimir E. Medenica, and Cathy J. Cohen. 2017. "Why 41 percent of White Millennials Voted for Trump." *Washington Post.* December 15. https://www.washingtonpost.com/news/monkey-cage/wp/2017/12/15/racial-resentment-is-why-41-percent-of-white-millennials-voted-for-trump-in-2016/?utm_term=.94335a7614da (last accessed by author on February 2, 2019).

Friedersdorf, Conor. 2016. "How the Party Decided on Trump." *The Atlantic.* May 3. https://www.theatlantic.com/politics/archive/2016/05/how-gop-influencers-cued-voters-to-choose-donald-trump/480294/ (last accessed by author on February 2, 2019).

Frey, William H. 2014. *Diversity Explosion: How New Racial Demographics Are Remaking America.* Washington, DC: Brookings Institution Press.

Frey, William H. 2017. "How Young Americans Are Set to Change the US Forever." *BBC,* July 17, 2017. https://www.bbc.com/news/world-us-canada-40461666. (last accessed by author on February 2, 2019).

Frey, William H. 2018a. "The U.S. Will Become 'Minority White' in 2045, Census Projects." *Brookings Institution,* March 14, 2018. https://www.brookings.edu/blog/the-avenue/2018/03/14/the-us-will-become-minority-white-in-2045-census-projects/. (last accessed by author on February 2, 2019).

Frey, William H. 2018b. "US Population Disperses to Suburbs, Exurbs, Rural Areas, and 'Middle of the Country' Metros." *Brookings Institution,* March 26, 2018. https://www.brookings.edu/blog/the-avenue/2018/03/26/us-population-disperses-to-suburbs-exurbs-rural-areas-and-middle-of-the-country-metros/. (last accessed by author on February 2, 2019).

Fuchs, Chris. 2018. "Before Obama, Asian Americans Voted Republican. The GOP Wants to Bring Them Back." *NBC News,* May 15, 2018. https://www.nbcnews.com/news/asian-america/obama-asian-americans-voted-republican-gop-wants-bring-them-back-n873401. (last accessed by author on February 2, 2019).

Gao, George. 2016. "Biggest Share of Whites in U.S. Are Boomers, But for Minority Groups It's Millennials or Younger." *Pew Research Center,* July 7, 2016. http://www.pewresearch.org/fact-tank/2016/07/07/biggest-share-of-whites-in-u-s-are-boomers-but-for-minority-groups-its-millennials-or-younger/. (last accessed by author on February 2, 2019).

Gest, Justin. 2016. *The New Minority: White Working Class Politics in an Age of Immigration and Inequality.* New York: Oxford University Press.

Gamboa, Suzanne, Mariana Atencio, and Gabe Gutierrez. 2018. "Why Are So Many Migrants Crossing the U.S. Border? It Often Starts with an Escape from Violence in Central America." *NBC News,* June 20, 2018. https://www.nbcnews.com/storyline/immigration-border-crisis/central-america-s-violence-turmoil-keeps-driving-families-u-s-n884956. (last accessed by author on February 2, 2019).

Gatins, Joseph, and Ed Briggs. 1978. "Churchmen See Future Alliances." *Richmond Times-Dispatch*, November 9.

Gayte, Marie, Blandine Chelini-Pont, and Mark J. Rozell, eds., *Catholics and US Politics After the 2016 Elections*. New York: Palgrave Macmillan, 2018.

Gerster, Patrick. 1989. "Religion and Mythology." In *The Encyclopedia of Southern Culture*, ed. Charles R. Wilson and William Ferris. Chapel Hill: University of North Carolina Press.

Gibson, Campbell, and Kay Jung. 2002. "Historical Census Statistics on Population Totals by Race, 1790 to 1990, and by Hispanic Origin, 1970 to 1990, for the United States, Regions, Divisions, and States." U.S. Census Bureau Population Division Working Paper No. 56. September 2002.

Gibson, Campbell and Kay Jung. 2006. "Historical Census Statistics on the Foreign-Born Population of the United States: 1850–2000." U.S. Census Bureau Population Division Working Paper No. 81. February 2006.

Gittinger, Ted, and Allen Fisher. 2007. "LBJ Champions the Civil Rights Act of 1964, Part 2." *Prologue Magazine* 36:2.

Gonino, Leanna. 2017. "Blacks' and Whites' Attitudes toward Race-Based Policies: Is There an Obama Effect?" *Michigan Sociological Review* 31: 173–188.

Green, John C., Mark J. Rozell, and Clyde Wilcox. 2001. "Social Movements and Party Politics: The Case of the Christian Right." *Journal for the Scientific Study of Religion* 40, no. 3: 413–426.

Greene, Melissa Faye. 1991. *Praying for Sheetrock*. Reading, MA: Addison-Wesley.

Gronke, Paul. 2004. "Early Voting Reforms and American Elections." Presented at the annual meeting of the American Political Science Association, Chicago, IL, September 2–5.

Grovum, Jake. 2014. "How Asian-Americans Are Changing the South." *Stateline*, October 3, 2014. https://www.pewtrusts.org/en/research-and-analysis/blogs/stateline/2014/10/03/how-asian-americans-are-changing-the-south. (last accessed by author on February 2, 2019).

Handley, Lisa, and Bernard Grofman. 1994. "The Impact of the Voting Rights Act on Minority Representation: Black Officeholding in Southern State Legislatures and Congressional Delegations." In *Quiet Revolution in the South*, ed. Chandler Davidson and Bernard Grofman. Princeton, NJ: Princeton University Press: 335–50.

Hardeman, D. B., and Donald C. Bacon. 1987. *Rayburn*. Austin: Texas Monthly Press.

Harvey, Paul. 2005. "Religion, Race, and the Right in the South, 1945–1990." In *Politics and Religion in the White South,* ed. Glenn Feldman. Lexington: University of Kentucky Press: 101–124.

Hofstadter, Richard. 1955. "The Pseudo-Conservative Revolt." In *The New American Right,* ed. Daniel Bell. New York: Criterion Books.

Holmes, Catesby. 2018. "5 Facts on Migrants Coming to the U.S." *U.S. News & World Report,* June 21, 2018. https://www.usnews.com/news/best-countries/articles/2018-06-21/why-are-central-americans-coming-to-the-united-states. (last accessed by author on February 2, 2019).

Holmes, Robert A. 1998. "Reapportionment Strategies in the 1990s: The Case of Georgia." In *Race and Redistricting in the 1990s,* ed. Bernard Grofman. New York: Agathon.

Hood, M. V., III, and Charles S. Bullock, III. 2012. "Much Ado about Nothing: An Empirical Assessment of the Georgia Voter Identification Statute." *State Politics and Policy Quarterly* 12: 394–414.

Hood, M. V., III, and Mark Caleb Smith. 2002. "On the Prospect of Linking Religious Right Identification with Political Behavior: Panacea or Snipe Hunt?" *Journal for the Scientific Study of Religion* 41: 697–710.

Hood, M. V., III, and Seth C, McKee. 2010. "What Made Carolina Blue? In-Migration and the 2008 North Carolina Presidential Vote." *American Politics Research* 38, no. 2: 266–302.

Hood, M. V., III, Quentin Kidd, and Irwin L. Morris. 2012. *The Rational Southerner*. New York: Oxford University Press.

Johnson, Melissa. 2018. "Southern States Must Build a Skilled Workforce for a Stronger Economy." *National Skills Coalition,* June 11, 2018. https://www.nationalskillscoalition.org/news/blog/southern-states-must-build-a-skilled-workforce-for-a-stronger-economy. (last accessed by author on February 2, 2019).

Ignatiev, Noel. 2008. *How the Irish Became White*. New York: Routledge.

Johnson, William R., and Derek Neal. 1998. "Basic Skills and the Black-White Earnings Gap." In *The Black-White Test Score Gap,* ed. Christopher Jencks and Meredith Phillips. Washington, DC: Brookings Institution Press, 480–497.

Jones, Ashley. 2009. Personal interview conducted by the author, November 9.

Kaiser Family Foundation. 2016. "Population Distribution by Race/Ethnicity." https://www.kff.org/other/state-indicator/distribution-by-raceethnicity/ ?currentTimeframe=0&sortModel=%7B%22colId%22:%22Location%22,% 22sort%22:%22asc%22%7D (last accessed by author on February 2, 2019).

Keech, William R. 1968. *The Impact of Negro Voting: The Role of the Vote in the Quest for Equality.* Chicago: Rand McNally.

Key, V. O., Jr. 1959. "Secular Realignment and the Party System." *Journal of Politics* 21 (May): 198–210.

Key, V. O., Jr. 1949. *Southern Politics in State and Nation.* New York: Knopf.

Knuckey, Jonathan. 2015. "The Myth of the 'Two Souths?' Racial Resentment and White Party Identification in the Deep South and Rim South." Presented at the annual meeting of the Southern Political Science Association, New Orleans, LA.

Kopf, Dan. 2016. "The Great Migration: The African American Exodus from the South." *Priceonomics*, January 28, 2016. https://priceonomics.com/the-great-migration-the-african-american-exodus/. (last accessed by author on February 2, 2019).

Kotkin, Joel. 2013. "How the South Will Rise to Power Again." *Forbes*, January 31, 2013. https://www.forbes.com/sites/joelkotkin/2013/01/31/how-the-south-will-rise-to-power-again. (last accessed by author on February 2, 2019).

Kotkin, Joel. 2015. "The Cities Where African-Americans Are Doing the Best Economically." *Forbes*, January 15, 2015. https://www.forbes.com/sites/ joelkotkin/2015/01/15/the-cities-where-african-americans-are-doing-the-best-economically. (last accessed by author on February 2, 2019).

Kranish, Michael, and Marc Fisher. 2016. *Trump Revealed: An American Journey of Ambition, Ego, Money, and Power.* New York: Scribner.

Kruse, Michael. 2016. "The True Story of Donald Trump's First Campaign Speech—in 1987." *Politico.* February 5.

Kuklinski, James H., Michael D. Cobb, and Martin Gilens. 1997. "Racial Attitudes and the 'New South.'" *The Journal of Politics* 59, no. 2, May: 323–349.

LaFrance, Adrienne. 2016. "Trump's Media Saturation, Quantified." *The Atlantic.* September 1. https://www.theatlantic.com/technology/archive/ 2016/09/trumps-media-saturation-quantified/498389/ (last accessed by author on February 2, 2019).

Lewis, John. 2002. Affidavit provided in *Georgia v. Ashcroft*, 195 F. Supp. 225 (D.D.C.).

Lipset, Seymour Martin, and Earl Raab. 1981. "The Election and the Evangelicals." *Commentary* 71: 25–32.

Livingston, Gretchen. 2017. "The Rise of Multiracial and Multiethnic Babies in the U.S." *Pew Research Center*, June 6, 2017. http://www.pewresearch.org/fact-tank/2017/06/06/the-rise-of-multiracial-and-multiethnic-babies-in-the-u-s/. (last accessed by author on February 2, 2019).

López, Gustavo, Kristen Bialik, and Jynnah Radford. 2018. "Key Findings about U.S. Immigrants." *Pew Research Center*, November 30, 2018. http://www.pewresearch.org/fact-tank/2018/11/30/key-findings-about-u-s-immigrants/. (last accessed by author on February 2, 2019).

López, Gustavo, Neil G. Ruiz, and Eileen Patten. 2017. "Key Facts about Asian Americans, A Diverse and Growing Population." *Pew Research Center*, September 8, 2017. http://www.pewresearch.org/fact-tank/2017/09/08/key-facts-about-asian-americans/. (last accessed by author on February 2, 2019).

Lopez, Mark Hugo, and Ana Gonzalez-Barrera. 2014. "Women's College Enrollment Gains Leave Men Behind." *Pew Research Center*, March 6, 2014. http://www.pewresearch.org/fact-tank/2014/03/06/womens-college-enrollment-gains-leave-men-behind/. (last accessed by author on February 2, 2019).

Lublin, David. 1997. *The Paradox of Representation*. Princeton, NJ: Princeton University Press.

MacManus, Susan A. 2017. *Florida's Minority Trailblazers: The Men and Women Who Changed Florida Government*. Gainesville: University Press of Florida.

Manley, John. 1973. "The Conservative Coalition." *American Behavioral Scientist* 17 (November –December): 225–230.

Martin, William. 1997. *With God on Our Side: The Rise of the Religious Right in America*. New York: Broadway Books.

Mayer, Jeremy D. 1996. Critical Mass: White Voters and Black Population Levels in the 1988 and 1992 Presidential Elections. PhD. Thesis, Georgetown University.

Mayer, Jeremy D. 2002. *Running on Race: Racial Politics in Presidential Campaigns 1960–2000*. New York: Random House.

Mayer, Jeremy D. 2004. "The Contemporary Presidency: The Presidency and Image Management: Discipline in Pursuit of Illusion." *Presidential Studies Quarterly* 34, no. 3: 620–31.

Mayer, Jeremy D. 2016. "Big Daddy Trump." *American Interest.* August 16. https://www.the-american-interest.com/2016/08/25/big-daddy-trump/ (last accessed by author on February 2, 2019).

McKee, Seth C. 2010. *Republican Ascendancy in Southern U.S. House Elections.* Boulder, CO: Westview Press.

McWhirter, Cameron. 2018. "Forget Florida: More Northern Retirees Head to Appalachia." *Wall Street Journal,* May 15, 2018. https://www.wsj.com/articles/forget-florida-more-northern-retirees-head-to-appalachia-1526388500. (last accessed by author on February 2, 2019).

Mendleberg, Tali. 2001. *The Race Card.* Princeton, NJ: Princeton University Press.

Miller, Derek. 2018. "Where Are Millennials Moving—2018 Edition." *SmartAsset,* June 12, 2018. https://smartasset.com/mortgage/where-are-millennials-moving-2018-edition. (last accessed by author on February 2, 2019).

Moore, Stephen. 2015. "High-Tailing It Out of Blue States." *Washington Times,* September 27, 2015. https://www.washingtontimes.com/news/2015/sep/27/stephen-moore-migration-changing-economy-of-us-sou/. (last accessed by author on February 2, 2019).

Neeley Grant W., and Lilliard E. Richadson, Jr. 2001. "Who is Early Voting? An Individual Level Examination." *Social Science Journal* 38: 381–392.

Nelson, Garrison. 1978. "The Matched Lives of U.S. House Leaders: An Exploration." Presented at the annual meeting of the American Political Science Association, New York, New York.

Oldfield, Duane Murray. 1996. *The Right and the Righteous: The Christian Right Confronts the Republican Party.* Lanham, MD: Rowman and Littlefield.

Ordoñez, Franco. 2015. "As Caribbean Immigration Rises, Miami's Black Population Becomes More Foreign." *McClatchy Washington Bureau,* April 10, 2015. https://www.mcclatchydc.com/news/nation-world/national/article24782917.html. (last accessed by author on February 2, 2019).

Page, Ann L., and Donald A. Clelland. 1978. "The Kanawha County Textbook Controversy: A Study of the Politics of Lifestyle Concern." *Social Forces* 57, no. 1: 265–281.

Patterson, Bill. 1977. "Fear Intense on Both Sides of Gay Rights Vote Tuesday." *Washington Post*, June 6.

Patterson, Thomas E. 1994. *Out of Order.* _____:Vintage Books.

Perez, Anthony Daniel, and Charles Hirschman. 2009. "The Changing Racial and Ethnic Composition of the US Population: Emerging American Identities." *Population Development Review* 35, no. 1 (March): 1–51.

Perry, Mark J. 2017. "Prediction: No 2017 Graduation Speaker Will Mention This—The Growing 'Gender College Degree Gap' Favoring Women." *AEI*, May 7, 2017. http://www.aei.org/publication/prediction-no-2017-graduation-speaker-will-mention-this-the-growing-gender-college-degree-gap-favoring-women/. (last accessed by author on February 2, 2019).

Petrocik, John R. and Scott Deposato. 1998. "The Partisan Consequences of Majority-Minority Redistricting in the South, 1992 and 1994." *Journal of Politics* 60 (August): 613–633.

Pew Research Center. 2015. "Modern Immigration Wave Brings 59 Million to U.S., Driving Population Growth and Change through 2065." September 28, 2015. http://www.pewhispanic.org/2015/09/28/modern-immigration-wave-brings-59-million-to-u-s-driving-population-growth-and-change-through-2065/. (last accessed by author on February 2, 2019).

Pew Research Center, 2019. "Religious Composition of Adults in the South". http://www.pewforum.org/religious-landscape-study/region/south/ (last accessed by author on January 27, 2019).

Phillips, Kevin P. 1969. *The Emerging Republican Majority.* New Rochelle, NY: Arlington House.

Proctor, Bradley. 2016. "An American 'Redemption'? Trumpism Fits a Pattern of Backlash against Social Progress." *Vox.* November 28. https://www.vox.com/the-big-idea/2016/11/28/13758392/second-american-redemption-trumpism (last accessed by author on February 2, 2019).

Reed, Ralph. 1994. *Politically Incorrect.* Dallas: Word Publishing.

Rodgers, Harrell, Jr., and Charles S. Bullock, III. 1972. *Law and Social Change.* New York: McGraw-Hill.

Rogerson, Peter. 2018. "America's Graying Population in 3 Maps." The Conversation, May 23, 2018. https://theconversation.com/americas-graying-population-in-3-maps-94344. (last accessed by author on February 2, 2019).

Rosenblum, Marc R., and Kate Brick. 2011. "U.S. Immigration Policy and Mexican/Central American Migration Flows: Then and Now." *Migration*

Policy Institute, August 2011. https://www.migrationpolicy.org/research/ RMSG-us-immigration-policy-mexican-central-american-migration-flows. (last accessed by author on February 2, 2019).

Rozell, Mark J. 2002. "The Christian Right in the 2000 GOP Presidential Campaign." In *Piety, Politics, and Pluralism: Religion, the Courts, and the 2000 Election*, ed. Mary Segers. Lanham, MD: Rowman and Littlefield: 57–74.

Rozell, Mark J., and Clyde Wilcox. 1995. *God at the Grassroots: The Christian Right in the 1994 Elections*. Lanham, MD: Rowman and Littlefield.

Rozell, Mark J., and Clyde Wilcox. 1997. *God at the Grassroots, 1996: The Christian Right in the 1996 Elections*. Lanham, MD: Rowman and Littlefield.

Rozell, Mark J., and Clyde Wilcox. 1996. *Second Coming: The New Christian Right in Virginia Politics*. Baltimore, MD: Johns Hopkins University Press.

Rozell, Mark J., and Debasree Das Gupta. 2006. "The 'Values Vote'? Moral Issues and the 2004 Elections." In *The Values Campaign? The Christian Right and the 2004 Elections*, ed. John C. Green, Mark J. Rozell, and Clyde Wilcox. Washington, DC: Georgetown University Press: 11–21.

Ruggles, Steven, Sarah Flood, Ronald Goeken, Josiah Grover, Erin Meyer, Jose Pacas, and Matthew Sobek. 2018. IPUMS USA: Version 8.0 [dataset]. Minneapolis, MN: IPUMS. https://doi.org/10.18128/D010.V8.0. (last accessed by author on February 2, 2019).

Schuman, Steeh, and Bobo. 1985. *Racial Attitudes in America: Trends and Interpretations*. Cambridge, MA: Harvard University Press.

Schuman, Howard, Charlotte Steeh, Lawrence Bobo, and Maria Krysan. 1997. *Racial Attitudes in America: Trends and Interpretations*. Revised Edition. Cambridge, MA: Harvard University Press.

Seitz-Wald, Alex. 2018. "NBC News Poll: The South, Once a Conservative Bastion, Is Changing." *NBC News*, April 12, 2018. https://www.nbcnews.com/politics/elections/nbc-news-poll-south-once-conservative-bastion-changing-n864441. (last accessed by author on February 2, 2019).

Serwer, Adam. 2016. "Is This The Second Redemption?" *The Atlantic*. November 10. https://www.theatlantic.com/politics/archive/2016/11/welcome-to-the-second-redemption/507317/ (last accessed by author on February 2, 2019).

Shaffer, Samuel. 1980. *On and Off the Floor*. New York: Newsweek Books.

Shelley, Mack C II. 1983. *The Permanent Majority: The Conservative Coalition in the United States Congress*. Tuscaloosa: University of Alabama Press.

Sides, J., M. Tesler, and L. Vavreck. 2018. *Identity Crisis: The 2016 Presidential Election and the Battle for the Meaning of America.* Princeton, NJ: Princeton University Press.

Silver, Nate. 2016. "The Republican Party May Be Failing." *538Politics.com.* January 25. https://fivethirtyeight.com/features/the-republican-party-may-be-failing/ (last accessed by author on February 2, 2019).

Sinclair, Barbara. 1982. *Congressional Realignment, 1925–1978.* Austin: University of Texas Press.

Skelley, Geoffrey. 2015. "Republicans 2016: White Evangelicals Dominate the Early Calender," *Sabato's Crystal Ball* (November 12), http://www.centerforpolitics.org/crystalball/articles/republicans-2016-white-evangelicals-dominate-the-early-calendar/ (last accessed by author on January 27, 2019).

Smidt, Corwin E., et al. 2009. *The Disappearing God Gap? Religion and the 2008 Presidential Election.* New York: Oxford University Press.

Stein, Robert M. 1998. "Early Voting." *Public Opinion Quarterly* 30: 53–57.

Talbot, Margaret. 2018. "The Women Running in the Midterms during the Trump Era." *The New Yorker,* April 18, 2018. https://www.newyorker.com/news/news-desk/2018-midterm-elections-women-candidates-trump. (last accessed by author on February 2, 2019).

Taylor, Paul, and Pew Research Center. 2016. *The Next America: Boomers, Millennials, and the Looming Generational Showdown.* New York: PublicAffairs.

Tesler, Michael. 2016. *Post-Racial or Most-Racial?: Race and Politics in the Obama Era.* Chicago: University of Chicago Press.

Tienda, Marta, and Susana M. Sánchez. 2013. "Latin American Immigration to the United States." *Daedalus* 142, no. 3 (Summer): 48–64.

Tindall, George Brown. 1976. *The Ethnic Southerners.* Baton Rouge: Louisiana State University Press.

Trevelyan, Edward. 2016. "Immigrant Voting in the United States." *U.S. Census Blogs,* November 30, 2016. https://www.census.gov/newsroom/blogs/random-samplings/2016/11/immigrant_votingin.html. (last accessed by author on February 2, 2019).

Tullos, Allen. 2011. *Alabama Getaway: The Political Imaginary and the Heart of Dixie.* Athens: University of Georgia Press.

West, Darrell M. 2018. "Trump Should Revive the Wealth Tax He Called for in 1999. America Needs It More than Ever." *USA Today.* July 31. https://www.

usatoday.com/story/opinion/2018/07/31/trump-1999-wealth-tax-lower-deficits-reduce-inequality-column/826224002/ (last accessed by author on February 2, 2019).

White, William S. 1956. *Citadel*. New York: Harper and Brothers.

Wilcox, Clyde, and Carin Larson. 2008. *Onward Christian Soldiers: The Religious Right in American Politics*. Boulder, CO: Westview Press.

Young et al.

Zitner, Aaron, and Anthony DeBarros. 2018. "The New Divide in Politics: Education." *Wall Street Journal*, November 10, 2018. https://www.wsj.com/articles/midterm-results-point-to-a-new-divide-in-politics-education-1541865601 (last accessed by author on February 2, 2019).

Index

Dornan, Bob, 111–12
Downs, Anthony, 100
Drezner, Dan, 130
Dukakis, Michael, 131–32
Durham (North Carolina), 88–89

early voting, 102–3
East, John, 79
Edwards, John, 116–17
Eisenhower, Dwight D., 5, 53, 54,
    58–59, 70, 80–81, 85–86
Engel v. Vitale, 110–11
Espy, Mike, 105–6
Evangelical Christians. *See also*
    Christian Right
    Democratic Party and, 13–14,
        115–16, 126–27, 156
    education policies and, 18
    election of 1976 and, 18, 110,
        155, 164n1
    election of 1980 and, 18, 112–13
    election of 1984 and, 114
    election of 1988 and, 114
    election of 1992 and, 115
    election of 2000 and,
        115–16, 118
    election of 2004 and,
        116–17, 118
    election of 2008 and, 117–18
    election of 2012 and, 118
    election of 2016 and Trump
        support among, 69, 70t, 119,
        156–57, 158
    Republican Party support among,
        3–4, 13–14, 18, 69, 96–97,
        98t, 110, 112–14, 115–19,
        125, 126–27, 155, 156

Fairfax, Justin, 96, 105–6
Falwell Jr., Jerry, 109
Falwell Sr., Jerry
    Evangelical Christians'
        involvement in politics and,
        18, 112–13, 155–56

McCain's comments during
    election of 2000
    regarding, 118
Reagan and, 112–13, 114
Republican Party and, 18
Farris, Michael, 123
Fields, Cleo, 92
Filipino Americans, 31, 32t
Florida
    African Americans in, 59–60, 62,
        69, 70t, 86–87, 89–91, 90t, 95,
        96, 98t, 105–6
    Asian Americans in, 31, 32t
    Congressional representation
        levels in, 7t
    Democratic Party gains during
        twenty-first century in, 6, 9–
        10, 17, 46, 71–72, 73, 74–75,
        76, 81, 151, 154
    educational attainment levels in,
        9t, 42f
    election of 1996 and, 115
    election of 2008 and, 13, 71–72,
        76, 117
    election of 2016 and, 10t, 69, 70t,
        71–72, 98t, 148
    election of 2018 and, 11,
        96, 105–6
    Evangelical Christians in, 69,
        70t, 98t
    foreign-born population in,
        25–26, 30
    Hispanics in, 3, 6, 15–16, 24, 28–29,
        29t, 59–60, 104–5
    largest industries in, 35t
    median family incomes in, 8t,
        43, 44f
    migration to and demographic
        change in, 3, 5–8, 13, 16, 22–
        23, 23t, 25–26, 30
    population growth levels in, 22–23,
        23t, 152
    redistricting in, 90t, 92–94
    Republican Party in, 6, 53

CPSIA information can be obtained
at www.ICGtesting.com
Printed in the USA
BVHW082253070120
568873BV00002B/12/P

9 780190 065928